Out of the Maelstrom

PSYCHOLOGY AND THE NOVEL IN THE TWENTIETH CENTURY

ALSO BY KEITH M. MAY

Aldous Huxley

Out of the Maelstrom

PSYCHOLOGY AND THE NOVEL IN THE TWENTIETH CENTURY

Keith M. May

Paul Elek London

To Nadine

First published in Great Britain 1977 by
Elek Books Limited
54–58 Caledonian Road, London N1 9RN

© 1977 Keith M. May

ISBN 0 236 40095 9

Printed in Great Britain by
Unwin Brothers Limited
The Gresham Press, Old Woking, Surrey

Contents

Acknowledgements

The author records his thanks to the following publishers and copyright holders for permissions to quote:
Martin Secker & Warburg Limited, and Alfred A. Knopf Inc., for an extract from Thomas Mann's *Past Masters and Other Papers*, translated by H. T. Lowe-Porter; Martin Secker & Warburg Limited for an extract from Franz Kafka's *Wedding Preparations in the Country*, translated by Ernst Kaiser and Eithne Wilkins; Schocken Books Inc., for an extract from *Dearest Father* (American edition of *Wedding Preparations in the Country*) by Franz Kafka, copyright © 1952 by Schocken Books Inc., translated by Ernst Kaiser and Eithne Wilkins; Laurence Pollinger Limited, William Heinemann Limited, the Cambridge University Press, the Viking Press Inc. and the estate of the late Mrs Frieda Lawrence for an extract from *The Letters of D. H. Lawrence*, edited by Aldous Huxley; Laurence Pollinger Limited, William Heinemann Limited, the Viking Press Inc. and the estate of the late Mrs Frieda Lawrence for extracts from D. H. Lawrence's *Fantasia of the Unconscious* and *Psychoanalysis and the Unconscious*; Harper & Row, Publishers, Inc. for an extract from Abraham H. Maslow's *Motivation and Personality*; Chatto & Windus Limited, Random House Inc. and the literary estate of C. K. Scott Moncrieff for an extract from Marcel Proust's *Swann's Way*, translated by C. K. Scott Moncrieff; Faber & Faber Limited for an extract from John MacMurray's *The Self as Agent*; the editors of *Encounter* for an extract from Iris Murdoch's 'Against Dryness'; George Allen & Unwin Limited and the Liveright Publishing Corporation for an extract from Sigmund Freud's *Introductory Lectures on Psycho-Analysis*, translated by Joan Riviere; the Hogarth Press Limited and the Liveright Publishing Corporation for an extract from Sigmund Freud's *The Future of an Illusion* in volume 21 of *The Complete Psychological Works of Sigmund Freud*; and the Hogarth Press Limited, Harcourt Brace Jovanovich Inc. and the literary estate of Virginia Woolf for an extract from Virginia Woolf's *Mrs Dalloway*.

Introduction

CONVERGENT ROADS

Virginia Woolf once remarked, with reference to the first post-impressionist exhibition in London, that 'In or about December, 1910 human character changed.'[1] She was only exaggerating, not fantasticating. She did not mean simply that conceptions of human character had changed, but neither, at the opposite extreme, was she denying that certain psychological laws endure, uniting modern people with Homer's Achaeans. Instead she was pointing to a modification of consciousness that, roughly speaking, consisted of a blurring of the distinction between subject and object, between the perceiver and the perceived. A kind of relativism had come into being, so that both the world at large and the processes of consciousness seemed less clearly defined and less systematically organized than of old. This book is about such psychological developments, and the particular change to which Virginia Woolf referred is part of the story.

Specifically it is about analogies between the observations of novelists and psychologists in the period since 1890. Apart from considerations of length and coherence there are other good reasons for restricting the scope of this study to one period, the modern, and to one literary form, the novel. In the nineteenth century psychology became increasingly separated from its parent discipline of philosophy, and increasingly self-conscious. By the turn of the century psychology had emerged as a fully-fledged, though sparsely represented, discipline, many of whose practitioners were little interested in current philosophical thought. Since that time some branches of psychology have become severely scientific, while others have continued to be quasi-philosophic. At one extreme there are the behaviourists; at the other the pioneer psycho-analysts, who carried on behaving like philosophers, at least to the extent of constructing value-systems, and those contemporary psychologists whose ideas derive from phenomenological philosophy. However, this is the century in which a vast amount of systematic study has been given to the mind itself, and in which some novelists (rather more than poets and playwrights) have tried, in the absence of an inherited external

vii

scheme, to extract meaning and value from the workings of minds.

I am speaking of a change of emphasis, rather than an absolute change, among a limited number of influential novelists in the twentieth century. What is probably an actual majority of leading European and American authors cannot be characterized in this way at all, because their explorations and criticisms have been largely confined to social and personal relationships, regarded without much difficulty as an end in themselves. Perhaps they are an end in themselves, but until recently it was not possible to see them in this way and the change from the old concepts of being (man as made in the image of God; man as subject to extra-human moral laws) has forced upon some important authors a type of exploration that other authors, some no less important, have been able to avoid. In this second type of author, as a rule, religion has been abandoned, embraced or disregarded fairly comfortably, so that the constitution of the human personality is not in itself a major problem.

What I have just been saying is true of Bennett and Galsworthy, of Dreiser and Steinbeck, of Pasternak and Solzhenitsyn. The categories of writing that these names represent will be confined to the margins of the picture, along with the work of certain schools of psychology. Of course it is possible, and it might well be profitable, to relate the findings of any group of psychologists to such novelists, though this would be to interpret them from the standpoint of psychology, which is not my intention. On the contrary, the object, or the preliminary object, is to investigate similarities between the deliberate aspirations of some novelists and those of some psychologists. The representatives of both groups will be those who have sought, or at the least have been disturbed by the absence of, comprehensive Meaning, formerly supplied by religious systems. These individuals—novelists or psychologists—were aware in varying degrees of environmental factors, but could not feel that their experience was adequately understood by reference to such factors. Thus Kafka knew all about alienation, but in spite of his socialism presumably would not have felt much enlightened by even the subtlest analyses of the alienating effects of modern urban life or of capitalism. In the same vein an instructive contrast may be observed between D. H. Lawrence and E. M. Forster: both men were perceptive about physical environments and movements of social history; but to Lawrence the ground of being was a sacred mystery, whereas to Forster a mystery was—as he often put it—just a muddle. Nevertheless it was Lawrence, rather more than Forster, who conducted a radical exploration of what he regarded as post-Christian human nature. On the other side of the fence Freud, simply because of his scientist's assumption that mysteries await our solutions and his belief that religion is a universal neurosis to be outgrown, must obviously be included. In short the test for inclusion of a novelist or a psychologist is whether he sees the mind or Being itself as the central problem to be investigated.

In examining some parallels between psychology and novels in the present century we shall not always be observing direct influences. Often enough the novelist will have found in the work of a psychologist concepts to match and extend his own intuitive insights, but occasionally a novelist will have worked in total ignorance or cavalier disregard of his counterpart in psychology. In any event, it is obvious that no creative writer does more than utilize and modify for his own purposes whatever he might find in scientific writings. Similarly a psychologist, or a certain type of psychologist, will merely draw upon works of fiction, regarding these as data to be set beside other data gathered in the consulting room, the hospital, or elsewhere. Direct influence of the one sort of worker upon the other seems to account for less than the simple fact that both worked in the same cultural conditions, which means that certain questions were imposed upon them by the age and that their answers fell within a particular range. The plainest form that this restriction takes is the light (brilliant though circumscribing) cast forward by the great philosopher, who is often the common precursor of both scientist and artist. Thus D. H. Lawrence's ideas sometimes resemble Jung's, not because Lawrence had read Jung (which he had) and been impressed by Jung (which he said he had not), but because each man was for a different personal reason engaged with what he saw as the need for a God both Dionysian and Apollonian to replace the purely Apollonian God whose death Nietzsche had announced.

The example of similarity between the ideas of Lawrence and Jung will serve also to indicate certain snares that it is necessary to circumvent in a book of this kind. Clearly the differences between these two men far outweigh the resemblances. Here, on the one hand, is Lawrence, about whom a great deal of exegetical and biographical work has been written, much of it devoted to teasing out the intricacies of his vision. There, on the other hand, is Jung, with his band of exponents to some extent disagreeing among themselves as they attempt to collate and clarify his varied explanations of, say, integration of the personality. The plain danger is that in abstracting elements in the thought of both men we shall put forward a supposed common denominator that both would have disowned. It is impossible to do more than attempt an accurate simplification of the psychologist and an exposition of the stance of the novelist that does not falsify the texture of his work.

The object of these activities is partly historical but it is mainly to clarify contemporary views of human nature and human possibilities. Historically a leading thread has to do with the notion of the unconscious mind, but this is viewed not as a means of throwing fresh light on the novelists (a familiar and by now much overworked approach) but as an enlargement of the concept of mind and as a means of closing the dualistic gap. Towards the end of the survey we have to reckon with the overthrow, or attempted overthrow, of the unconscious.

To begin just before the beginning, consider George Eliot and G. H. Lewes working side by side in the mid 1870s, she producing *Daniel Deronda*, he his *Problems of Life and Mind* (published posthumously in 1879). I select George Eliot because of all English novelists of the pre-modern period she was the most interested in psychology, and *Daniel Deronda* because it was her last and in some respects most 'modern' novel. Lewes was at the forefront of contemporary psychological thinking in England, being chiefly associated with Spencer and Mill, though there were fundamental disagreements.

Lewes's psychology was firmly rooted in biology and at the same time was much concerned with social factors. It was at once thoroughly Victorian and in some respects quite modern. There was little sense of the mind as a separable entity and no conception of the mind as having regions inaccessible to normal observation. Lewes's psychology, in other words, was in harmony with those mid-twentieth-century schools (some highly scientific, others existentialistic) which replace 'mind' by behaviour and disown the unconscious. We have come full circle, but learned much in the meantime.

Perhaps chief among George Eliot's talents was her mastery of what is now known as 'ego-psychology': how expert she was on the mechanisms of defence, not least in *Daniel Deronda*! The heroine, Gwendolen Harleth, constitutes an excellent study of a moderately 'schizoid' personality, though Deronda himself is a less satisfactory (because zealously contrived) portrait of what some latter-day psychologists (notably the American, Abraham Maslow) call 'self-actualization'. But in its treatment of individual psychology *Daniel Deronda* is almost entirely confined to mental activities that either are, or with better insight could be, perfectly within the grasp of the characters. Certainly there are strange mental states in the book, such as Gwendolen's nervous reactions or the pre-visions of the fervent Jew, Mordecai, but these are mentioned rather than diagnosed. There is little sense of a missing dimension: there could not be, because George Eliot had never heard of the 'unconscious' in its twentieth-century meaning. It is left to the modern biographer of George Eliot to suggest that Gwendolen's physical aversion to men (not only to Grandcourt, her husband, but also to the wholesome, engaging Rex Gascoigne) might indicate latent homosexuality in her.[2] This suggestion is entirely typical of our own time, and entirely untypical of George Eliot's, in its assumption that physical aversion can be explained, needs to be explained, and probably will be explained by reference to unconscious factors.

A simple summary of what I am saying about G. H. Lewes and George Eliot, those two leaders of thought in their period, is that they were interested in conscious behaviour and socially optimistic. An equally simple (though this time, no doubt, too simple) summary of what I shall be saying about a prominent thread in the following period is that consciousness becomes burdensomely intensive and accompanied by a sense of unknown mental hinterlands. Late Hardy includes, as a variant of lifelong pessimism, the phenomenon of Sue Bridehead, who is at once torturedly conscious and impelled by forces that neither she nor her author fully understands. Conrad's characters are loyal or weak or vicious in the face of strange upheavals or cruelties; James's intricate analyses are rooted in what he termed an 'imagination of disaster'; in Mann the more a character reflects upon himself the more his fate is determined by dissociated impulses; Kafka's extraordinary but also representative talent was, in his own words, 'for portraying my dreamlike inner life'.

One important thing that was happening concurrently in the field of psychology was the emergence of the concept of the unconscious. It was not a new concept, for some indeed trace its origins back to Aristotle, and in the nineteenth century Schopenhauer and Eduard von Hartmann had been prominent among those who postulated the existence of unconscious drives. But, of course, it was the psycho-analysts' version of the unconscious that swiftly seized hold of people's imaginations.

Of the three major early figures in psycho-analysis, Adler said comparatively little about the unconscious; Jung said a great deal that was at once original and profoundly traditional, and Freud produced ideas that have few rivals for pure originality in the history of thought. Freud's ideas were the most widely disseminated among psychologists and the intellectual public, including novelists, and these ideas provided a detour (I do not imply a false or harmful detour) while Jung's and Adler's were in philosophical descent from, among others, Schopenhauer, Nietzsche and Hartmann.

As is well known, the starting point of Freud's ideas was not philosophical enquiry but observation of Charcot's patients in the winter of 1885–6. From these observations (in particular the production and removal of hysterical symptoms by hypnosis) came the theory of repression. Freud wrote: 'We obtain our concept of the unconscious from the theory of repression.'[3] By the time of the *Introductory Lectures on Psycho-Analysis* (1915–17) Freud had constructed the following account of the unconscious: first there is the innate unconscious, the whole mind of the infant, upon which consciousness gradually supervenes, and secondly there are elements which, through incompatibility with conscious attitudes, are forced into the unconscious. These latter elements are dynamic until they are brought back into the conscious processes.

Freud believed in psychological, as opposed to philosophical, determinism. He was a rationalist who thought that free will was possible to the extent that the unconscious could be eliminated: 'Where id was, there shall ego be.' But to writers and other artists, and indeed to all individuals who were shocked by twentieth-century revelations of human nature, Freud's system of ideas can be seen in retrospect to have been both a boon and a curse. For precisely in the period that the *Introductory Lectures on Psycho-Analysis* were being delivered at Vienna University, there was taking place in Flanders the most convincing demonstration that facilely optimistic views of human nature needed to be revised; that, in short, Freud's ideas about unconscious motivations (or something like those ideas) had to be embraced. It is in this sense that Freudianism was a boon to some writers in the twenties and thirties: it provided not only a gold mine of motifs but also an explanation (in circumstances where explanation was desperately needed) of the fact that barbarities did not belong to the distant past in Europe.

But Freudianism was a curse to writers and artists insofar as it placed severe restrictions on human possibilities. The system was evolutionistic in advocating the conquest of unreason by reason, but dispiriting because what was thought of as the well-spring of creative activity was precisely what it was deemed necessary to destroy. What happened, therefore, was that many writers availed themselves of material thrown up by Freud's researches, while ignoring (perhaps very sensibly) those of Freud's views that apparently postulated, as an ultimate objective, the abandonment of art. But this sort of accommodation could not continue for very long, since sooner or later any writer serious enough to come to grips with leading threads of contemporary thought could not avoid being perturbed by a belief that his own vocation belonged (like religion) to the infancy of the human race. He was bound to suspect, also, that his own finer moments of perception, however irrational in their origins, might be every bit as useful as pure reason in furthering man's development. Freud's theories, as we shall see, were also a means of explaining man's sense of alienation from the natural scheme (as expressed for example, in Hardy and Kafka), and they indicated a path of re-integration, but paradoxically they also emphasized the distance between subject and object, the investigator and the field of his investigations. It was D. H. Lawrence who vigorously pointed out this deficiency and who further maintained that there was a 'true unconscious' lying deeper than the Freudian unconscious, from which the all-important individuality of living things takes its rise. Lawrence was against Freud and rather scornful of Jung; yet his views had much in common with Jung's.

Perhaps the single most important difference, at least from the writer's point of view, between Freud and Jung is that the latter regarded the unconscious as an everlasting and valuable constituent of the psyche. To Jung it was not a kind of receptacle whose contents could gradually and profitably be emptied into consciousness, but a collection of forces complementary to those found in consciousness. The Jungian unconscious, while including Freud's 'preconscious' and whatever attitudes might have been morbidly repressed, consisted also of 'archetypes' and tendencies of an opposing nature to those found in the conscious mind. The proper objective was not the eradication of the unconscious (which was impossible, anyway) but a fruitful collaboration between conscious and unconscious forces.[4] On reaching or nearly approaching this objective a man would be a saint rather than a great artist, no doubt, but something like the Jungian view of the matter many artists down the ages must have obscurely felt to be true.

So far, in giving this outline of some interactions or parallel developments between literature and psychology from the end of the last century to the early decades of the present century, I have suggested that the sequence consisted of, first, a recognition (sometimes tacit, often obscure) by a limited number of writers that the old explanations of behaviour were inadequate, followed by scientists' accounts of the nature of the unconscious, followed in turn by creative writers' exploitations—or, in some instances, denunciations —of these scientific discoveries. The next stage, I shall contend, was initiated by literary men, and it consisted of a growing awareness of problems of personal identity.

Problems of this kind have always been with us, more prominently in some periods of history than in others, but of course we are now concerned with the peculiarly modern varieties. It is true, also, that there were earlier philosophical considerations of modern identity problems—in Bergson's *Time and Free Will*, for example, in Bradley's *Appearance and Reality*, not to mention the enveloping field of existentialism from Kierkegaard onwards—but direct, focused excursions into these questions were pioneered by such novelists as Proust and Virginia Woolf. These two writers were remarkably ahead of their time in that, while working in the period of Freud's greatest impact, and while absorbing Freud's ideas, they had much that was fresh to give to the next generation of writers and psychologists. It is notable how often latter-day psychologists draw upon not only Proust and Virginia Woolf, but also such figures as Elizabeth

Bowen, Camus, Koestler, Carson McCullers, Ortega Y Gasset, to bolster their own observations of health and pathology. One recurrent concern in these writers is the creation and maintenance of a sense of identity, whether in the drawing-room or in more plainly desperate situations. The psychologist Helen Merrell Lynd sums up this development when she writes:

> So great has been the impact of the changes of recent years that it is possible for an innovating Freudian psychoanalyst, Erik H. Erikson, to say that the search for identity has become as strategic in our time as the study of sexuality was in Freud's time.[5]

For this post-Freudian generation of artists and scientists the unconscious has simply been assimilated; the 'Shadow' side of man's nature (to adapt the Jungian terminology) may be a source of dismay, but not of bewilderment. If there are inexplicable extra dimensions, these are the property of science fiction and parapsychology, rather as they were to Wells, Conan Doyle, and Sir Oliver Lodge.

Now, of course, for the hero of a fiction to experience identity problems is, in the broad sense, part of a tradition in Western literature from Sophocles onwards, and certainly many a novel since the beginnings of the novel-form has turned on a question of identity. But once the questions were primarily social or familial: who were the hero's parents? to which social class does he belong? We can detect a gradual shift from the 'outer' mystery to the 'inner', from 'who am I?' to 'what sort of a person am I?' as the nineteenth century progressed. In *Great Expectations*, for example, it is still primarily a matter of class, of whether Pip is or is not a gentleman, but Pip's moral nature (unlike Tom Jones's in an earlier generation) is deeply affected. But in George Eliot, our representative of the following generation to Dickens's, the concern is overwhelmingly about moral and vocational choice—class is a secondary matter. It is often necessary for characters to come to know themselves by reflecting on the choices they have made in the spheres of personal relationships and professional occupations. To recall our earlier example, Daniel Deronda himself has mysterious origins, and his progress in self-knowledge is bound up with access to information about his parentage, but the Deronda theme is a study in creative self-fulfilment, to which orientation to a group (the Jews) is subsidiary.

What the early modernistic novelists had to do, as we have seen, was to apprehend (as a rule by oblique methods) the more obscure driving forces that, as had become apparent, were present in everyone. Once this had been partly accomplished, the next task was to wrestle with problems of identity in circumstances of extraordinary flux and complexity. On the one hand, looking inwards, the individual felt obliged to acknowledge that his ego was only a fraction of his total psychic make-up; and on the other hand, looking outwards, he saw rapidly shifting social and environmental patterns. He could no longer conclude either that he was purely and simply what he seemed to himself and others to be, or that he would necessarily enjoy permanent membership of a particular group, class or nation. On the whole it can be said that earlier writers and psychologists stressed the inner problems, while later writers and psychologists emphasize the outer relationships, though there has been and still is considerable overlapping.

Our summary has now reached the (still continuing) phase in which social concerns predominate in the novel, as they did for George Eliot, but with greater awareness of the roots of conduct than was available to the Victorians. There has been a spiralling upwards, in terms of theoretical knowledge if not of literary quality, so that contemporary perceptions profitably include the fruits of early twentieth-century excursions into the subjective and the irrational.

But within the last twenty years or so a fresh development has taken place. We are moving, I believe, around another turn of the spiral with psychologists at present in the lead, though the movement was initiated by French writers in the period from the late thirties to about 1950. The development began—if it can be said to have begun at any exact point—with the publication in 1938 of Jean-Paul Sartre's *La Nausée* and was consolidated in 1943 by Sartre's *L' Etre et le Néant*. The latter work included, as part of the author's thesis in favour of free will, an attack on a version of Freud's conception of the unconscious. It will later be necessary to examine Sartre's view in some detail, but for the moment it is sufficient to say that the attack was concentrated on the location of the Freudian 'censor' (is it or is it not an element in the conscious mind?) and that both philosophers and psychologists have often counter-attacked, declaring that Sartre misrepresented Freud and conducted a spurious argument on the basis of his misrepresentations. Just the same it was from this beginning, and of course under the influence of Sartre's work as a whole, especially the novels and plays, that the schools of existential psychology arose. Two important features of these schools, from our point of view, are the relative lack of attention paid to the unconscious mind and the pervading optimism. If Sartre failed to prove the non-existence of the psycho-analytical unconscious, many psychologists influenced by Sartre's analyses of mind have behaved as if he did. They write as though a man's moral and spiritual nature is in fact a product of the choices he (most of the time unwittingly) makes. The unconscious has been all but replaced by Sartre's notion of 'bad faith'.

Thus far it may be said that contemporary novelists and psychologists are keeping pace with each other, but lately there has arisen in psychology rather than in literature a new kind of evolutionary optimism. One common feature of the work of such diverse figures as Allport and Maslow, Erikson, Fromm and Frankl is the resurrection in a new form of the old belief that any man by taking thought can add a cubit to his stature. All dwell on the possibilities of self-enhancement in ways that would have been out of place in the Freudian generation and are still missing from much (but not all) contemporary fiction. It is contended that an impulse to personal growth is implanted within all individuals and instead of being a sublimation of instinctive drives has itself something of the nature of an instinct. Self-choice in a sense that is partly Lawrentian and partly existentialistic is increasingly recognized. What seems to have happened is that the dour stoicism of French existentialists during and just after the last war provided a shaping force, but the tone of the challenge entailed by notions of 'contingency' and 'absurdity' has changed from grim to exhilarating. But this change, I repeat, is more apparent in the ranks of humanistic psychologists than among novelists. From the former it is possible to build up a picture of a sort of hero who bears some resemblance to traditional 'good' men, who is frequently joyful but is nevertheless not shallow, conformist or lacking in individuality. Yet, it should be emphasized, some of these psychologists have been imbued with Freud's ideas and are not now in any radical way reacting against Freud but building on Freudian foundations in a fresh way. The final part of this book is a commentary on the contemporary novel in the light of these psychologists' views and an attempt to define an influential latter-day concept of man.

1

THE BURDEN
OF CONSCIOUSNESS

Freud and the European Novel at the Turn of the Century

Today we occupy a good vantage point from which to examine certain literary features of the turn of the century. Our age emphasizes immediacy and spontaneity, and our communications media, according to Marshall McLuhan and his followers, foster aural and tactile rather than visual responses, spatial rather than linear modes of apprehension. We have an abundance of drama, some of which is conspicuously unconcerned with intellectual analysis, and our novels tend to be dramatic in form. There is widespread interest in Zen, Yoga, Buddhism and oriental art. In short, in one way or another, we frequently (and no doubt clumsily) strive to close the gap between observer and observed, between subject and object, between the 'I' and the 'not-I'.

But at the end of the nineteenth century novelists were highly aware of themselves as observers directing attention upon their subject-matter. The Naturalists concentrated 'scientifically' on aspects of the environment and on human behaviour in relation to the environment. Zola even thought of himself as conducting experiments, somewhat in the manner of a scientist. He wrote: 'We are, in a word, experimental moralists, showing by experiment in what way a passion acts in certain social conditions.'[1] The novelists I shall be dealing with in this chapter were not impressed with Naturalism, but for all their differences from Zola and his school we can detect one underlying similarity. Zola was interested in behaviour; some other writers were interested in the nature of man's being, but all took it for granted that the problem of man had to be solved, or at least faced, by the reflective consciousness. Perhaps the simplest way to put the matter is to say that it was common to

1

see a difference between living and understanding the process of living. To understand it was necessary to stand back, to contemplate in some fashion. Today there is a common assumption that understanding of a sort is reached through barely reflective involvement.

We are dealing with a period in which for some writers man had himself become the problem, in the ontological as well as the merely social or moral sense, because the old religious model was in disrepair. Increasingly cut off from the world of nature, increasingly persuaded that the loftiest activities of his own mind were not excelled anywhere in the universe, man (unless of an optimistic scientific persuasion) felt himself to be excessively vulnerable and charged with tasks beyond his capacity. Obviously we—in the 1970s—have not moved into calmer waters, but advances of a sort have been made and we confront the problem in a different way. It is unlikely, for example, that a contemporary author would express himself as Thomas Hardy did in making the following comment on the character of Clym Yeobright in *The Return of the Native*:

> He already showed that thought is a disease of flesh, and indistinctly bore evidence that ideal physical beauty is incompatible with emotional development and a full recognition of the coil of things. Mental luminousness must be fed with the oil of life, even though there is already a physical demand for it; and the pitiful sight of two demands on one supply was just showing itself here.[2]

Clym Yeobright is what Hardy calls a 'modern' type, and Hardy is here contrasting the late nineteenth century with earlier periods in which, he assumed, it was possible to combine ideal physical beauty with emotional development. Hardy's view was that the most 'advanced' individual, the person most aware of the 'coil of things' *now*, in a fairly late phase of industrialization and after the message of Darwin had sunk in, was bound to bear the marks of mental anguish. Only the relatively obtuse, the emotionally stunted, the deluded, could escape this particular fate.

In fact the matter in Hardy is more complicated than I have so far indicated, but what Hardy is expressing through Clym Yeobright will serve as an instance of what I am calling 'the burden of consciousness', the feeling that it is both imperative and debilitating to be fully alive to one's nature and the nature of the world. Such an attitude clearly rests on a sense of distinction, if not opposition, between the consciousness of the individual and that of which he is conscious. He is here and the world is over there. Nature is not in tune with his aspirations; social customs jar against his feelings; his relationships with other people are prickly or perverse; his own 'lower' instincts, if acknowledged at all, are at variance with his 'finer' impulses. The obvious contrast with this condition is the Hellenic condition (mentioned in more than one novel by Hardy) in which zestful thought and regard for beauty managed to co-exist. The modern world, however, cannot engender anything resembling the Hellenic harmony, because man's consciousness has leaped ahead of the rest of nature.

This, with local modifications, is Hardy's position when he is at his most pessimistic—in *The Return of the Native*, *Tess of the D'Urbervilles* and *Jude the Obscure*. In the first of these three tragedies, the hero, Clym Yeobright, survives, but in a sad, diminished way. He loses Eustacia Vye, through her affair with Damon Wildeve and her death by drowning; temporarily he becomes almost blind; he becomes a furze-cutter, and finally an itinerant preacher. Those in the novel who die, Eustacia, Wildeve, and Mrs Yeobright, do so through their failure to adapt to Egdon Heath; while those who survive, Diggory Venn and Thomasin Yeobright, along with Clym, do so by merging with the landscape. It has always been recognized that the Heath is a microcosm, not just a topographical peculiarity in Dorset, so that Hardy was expressing his conviction that man's aspirations are liable to be brought down by natural forces, of which man is himself a product. It does not matter fundamentally whether the aspirations are cheap and shallow, like Wildeve's, grand though anachronistic, like Eustacia's, or 'advanced' and 'noble' like Clym's: people must bring their desires in line with external necessity, and this is felt as a matter for regret.[3]

But we are concerned primarily with Clym's form of hubris, the hubris of awareness. The Hardeian view is that 'thought is a disease of flesh'. Clym's consciousness is on one side of the barrier while his body belongs on the other side with the rest of the natural order. Energy given to thought is inevitably subtracted from the body. There is nothing new in this notion, which obviously contains some truth, but Hardy represents Clym's brand of ennervating thought as inevitable for the best people in modern times. This is the consequence of man's uniqueness in the natural scheme; the uniqueness, that is, of his greatly developed consciousness. In the absence of a benevolent God he must take upon himself awesome responsibilities, even though he is relatively powerless. Nature is all-powerful but blind, while man is frail but discerning, and man is impelled to understand what he cannot transform. The part is greater in wisdom than the whole. So the modern man, such as Clym, can only fret and allow his body (which stands apart from his consciousness) to waste away.

Other modern characters in Hardy, such as Angel Clare, Jude Fawley and Sue Bridehead, manifest the same condition. Hardy describes Angel Clare, the son of a Low Church parson, as an 'advanced and well-meaning young man', who is 'yet the slave to custom and conventionality when surprised back into his early teachings'.[4] In the light of Clare's behaviour this seems to be a perfectly accurate description. He revolts against an orthodox clerical career, such as his father dearly wished for him, becomes a farm-worker and so meets Tess at Talbothays dairy. He is a reader, a thinker, who discredits what Hardy calls the 'old systems of mysticism', but retains a desire to help mankind. So it is as a kind of post-Darwinian humanist that Angel courts and marries Tess, but it is the residue of his childhood training that produces such horror in him when Tess makes her confession about Alec d'Urberville. Later when he is in Brazil he comes to discard the 'old appraisements of morality' as well, and ends, after Tess's execution, a grief-stricken figure, fully alive to the miseries of the modern world. Of course, it is very much to the point that Clare has always been restless and searching, as is inevitable, in Hardy's view, for a sensitive young man of the time. Clare's earlier idealization of Tess, his general readiness to construct theoretical models of persons and activities rather than assimilate plain facts, is part of the latter-day yearning on the part of some of the best young people to find a substitute for the vanished sense of the divine.

The role of Nature is immense in the *Return of the Native* and *Tess of the D'Urbervilles*, but is quite diminished in *Jude the Obscure*. Tess was a 'natural' person, 'pure' in the sense of having spontaneous, well-intentioned impulses (though experiencing the 'ache of modernism'), but the most natural character in *Jude* is the coarse-grained Arabella Donn. The figures who receive Hardy's sympathy, Jude, Sue Bridehead and Phillotson, are aspiring, bookish, intellectual, on the whole divorced from Nature. *Jude* is about man trying to get along without Nature, without the sanction and security of old customs, without more than minimal or sporadic reliance on instinct. The three main characters exhibit different forms of alienation from Nature: Phillotson is a conscientious man (perhaps heroically so); Jude is provided with no means of steadily reconciling his sensual appetites with his spiritual leanings; Sue confusedly attempts to force her energies away from the gross flesh 'up' to the 'higher centres' of emotion and thought.

Sue is the true intellectual of the book, for Jude is a scholar—of what potential quality it is not easy to be sure—and Phillotson has a schoolmaster's nature. Sue, for all her bad faith and power to exasperate, is actually brilliant, original, the most daring mind in Hardy. Through her, yet again, Hardy aims to show the fallacy of resurrecting pre-Christian concepts in post-Christian times, for Sue's 'pagan' notions are dashed by her experiences in the conditions of the nineties. The Hardeian version of the burden of

4

consciousness is most completely expressed in Sue because her thoughts run the gamut from a dream of consonance between man and his world to a recognition of a nearly perfect dissonance.

Vague and quaint imaginings had haunted Sue in the days when her intellect scintillated like a star, that the world resembled a stanza or melody composed in a dream; it was wonderfully excellent to the half-aroused intelligence, but hopelessly absurd at the full waking; that the First Cause worked automatically like a somnambulist, and not reflectively like a sage; that at the framing of the terrestrial conditions there seemed never to have been contemplated such a development of emotional perceptiveness among the creatures subject to those conditions as that reached by thinking and educated humanity.[5]

A blunt way of putting this would be to say that man's consciousness is the latest phase of evolutionary development, the beginnings of which were unconscious. But the central and interesting notion is, of course, that consciousness has, in some people, outstripped its physical environment. More precisely, there is an implicit dualism in the passage, for man's 'emotional perceptiveness' is assumed to be merely 'subject' to 'terrestrial conditions' rather than—as the thoroughgoing monist would allege—an aspect of those conditions. Here is the root of the burden of consciousness, in the belief that because consciousness can reflect upon things it must be completely different from whatever it studies—a difference rendered tolerable only by the belief that a higher consciousness governs all.

Sue Bridehead eventually becomes a Christian, but her conversion, far from being a solution, is part of the tragic outcome of the novel. At Jude's last meeting with Sue he, referring to her penitential return to her husband, Phillotson, talks of her 'melancholy wreck of a promising human intellect'. The implication, which is Hardy's as well as Jude's, is that the only alternative to a deliberate blunting of intellectual power is death. Sue has been crushed partly by convention, or—according to Hardy's emphasis—by the terrestrial conditions that enjoin upon every animal some degree of co-operation with the rest of the pack. So the intellect is not free, but how else can it function?

But more or less contemporaneously with *Jude the Obscure* another way of looking at the matter was being explored by the early psycho-analysts. Freud's outlook was of course not tragic, though he derived much sustenance from tragedy, and as a scientist and medical practitioner he regarded the problem, which Hardy faced stoically, as capable of solution. Both Hardy and Freud were, in their strikingly different ways, evolutionists. To Hardy, Sue Bridehead and Jude Fawley were creatures ahead of their time in the evolutionary scheme, sensitized beyond the level permitted by late nineteenth-century conditions. Freud, however, in the first of the *Introductory Lectures on Psycho-Analysis*, expressed what is essentially the same problem in the following way:

> We believe that civilization has been built up, under the pressure of the struggle for existence, by sacrifices in gratification of the primitive impulses, and that it is to a great extent for ever being re-created, as each individual, successively joining the community, repeats the sacrifice of his instinctive pleasures for the common good. The sexual are amongst the most important of the instinctive forces thus utilized: they are in this way sublimated, that is to say, their energy is turned aside from its sexual goal and diverted towards other ends, no longer sexual and socially more valuable. But the structure thus built up is insecure, for the sexual impulses are with difficulty controlled; in each individual who takes up his part in the work of civilization there is a danger that a rebellion of the sexual impulses may occur, against this diversion of their energy.[6]

The context of these remarks is Freud's attempt to persuade his audience of the truth of two startling tenets of psycho-analysis: that 'mental processes are essentially unconscious'[7] and that 'sexual impulses have contributed invaluably to the highest cultural, artistic, and social achievements of the human mind'.[8] The truly revolutionary assertion was the second rather than the first, for while people had long entertained the idea of some form of unconscious 'thought' or impulses, they had earlier encountered only fitful and unsystematic demonstrations that their highest activities somehow depended on their lowest.[9] The crux in *Jude the Obscure* is the irreconcilability of high and low impulses, but Freud a few years later was maintaining that the high was derived from the low. Freud's notion has since become in one way commonplace and in another way perverted, for everyone knows about 'sublimation', though not everyone realizes that Freud was, so to speak, in favour of it. After the first impact of Freudianism the idea fairly rapidly got about that to sublimate sexual drives into some spiritual activity, for instance, was a false step. But Freud himself, as is clear from the above passage, regarded sublimation as the sole and admirable cause of civilization. It follows that Freud, far from exhorting a Sue Bridehead to behave like an Arabella Donn, would at least have respected the aspirations of a Sue Bridehead. Of course he would also have regretted what he would have regarded as her ignorance of the facts of psychic life. In

6

the novel Sue's attempt is to transcend the terrestrial conditions framed by a somnambulistic First Cause, but this, in the Freudian view, can be done with the fewest pathological consequences by first recognizing that noble wishes grow from ignoble subterranean impulses, that the flower has its life-giving roots in the dung.

Freud's own life's work was a massive spiritual enterprise aimed, quite obviously, at pushing man up the evolutionary ladder. Consciousness would grow and cease to be burdensome by acknowledging the unconscious; reason would be strengthened by understanding the irrational. In the Hardeian vision our finer perceptions are disconnected from—and therefore in apparent hostility to—the laws of Nature, whereas in the Freudian view an unbroken line runs from human perception to natural law through the territory of the unconscious. There is no actual gulf, only an imaginary one produced by generations of ignorant endeavour. Freud's pronouncement of the existence of the unconscious and his description of its dynamic processes can usefully be seen as an argument against the modern forms of Manichaeism. The ancient Manichees held that spirit, the good principle, is separate from matter, the embodiment of the evil principle, and any latter-day assumption that the material universe, including the human body, impedes the human spirit, can surely be related to this doctrine. Freud's arguments (or findings) constituted an assertion that what we call spirit is wholly dependent on matter. In relation to our immediate theme Freud's ideas tended to show that consciousness in his period had become a torment as a result of disowning its instinctual foundations. The way back to Nature was through the unconscious.

Paradoxically, a writer who seems to have sensed this avenue of progress was Henry James, the arch-observer of the intricacies of consciousness. I do not suggest that the Freudian unconscious plays any conspicuous role in James's fiction (if we leave aside such considerations as the Freudian interpretation of 'The Turn of the Screw'), but simply that his most satisfactory works reveal an interdependence of moral good and bad, of the noble endeavour and the stain of corruption. Here is an ethical emphasis that begins by taking almost for granted what Hardy in his later works found almost intolerable—that our best yearnings are clogged by mundane, and sometimes vicious, factors. Hardy's Tess is brought down because of her natural purity: she has no guile, no worldliness. Presumably the 'President of the Immortals' invested her with such purity and then for his sport provided snares that only an impure woman could circumvent. Jude, likewise, is a kind of impractical innocent. In these works Hardy seems to be regretting the need to take practical, calculating steps to fulfil one's desires, because such steps corrupt the desires.

7

James, on the other hand, while regretfully accepting the same conditions, tried to celebrate corrupted, rather than pure, heroism. His muse is tragic because the heroes and heroines (apart from Milly Theale in *The Wings of the Dove*) bravely survive in some impure state. In this way James, without knowing about Freud's theories, anticipated the moral concerns that those theories (among other factors) foisted on later generations. If good and bad are inextricably bound up together, how shall we know what to strive for? If, for example, active concern for one's fellow men really is a sublimated form of sadism, as Freud seems to have implied, does this invalidate or in some degree pollute the concern?

James in his best fiction squarely faced the modern problem of moral ambiguity, so striding ahead of all those Victorian productions, great and small, in which some characters are good by nature or attain to a barely qualified goodness. In James there are no equivalents to Dickens's Joe Gargery or Lizzie Hexham, to George Eliot's Dinah Morris or Dorothea Brooke, to Hardy's Gabriel Oak or Giles Winterbourne.

An excellent illustration of James's modernism is provided by a comparison between *The Portrait of A Lady* and George Eliot's *Daniel Deronda*, for, as Leon Edel has pointed out in the biography of James, '*The Portrait* was Henry's way of making Isabel Archer the personality he felt George Eliot should have made of Gwendolen Harleth.'[10] It is not of course that Isabel is 'worse' than Gwendolen, but simply that Isabel survives in a loveless relationship with Gilbert Osmond and his daughter, Pansy, while Gwendolen, having murdered her husband in her heart, ends in what George Eliot regarded as a proper state of penitence. George Eliot found it necessary to offset the corrupt world of Grandcourt and Gwendolen by a world of altruism represented in the figures of Mirah, Mordecai and Daniel Deronda himself. Mirah, indeed, is, apart from the odd moment of jealousy, a paragon such as James would never have contrived. In *The Portrait* there are no pure people (only ordinarily decent ones such as Warburton) and the implication of the novel is not that Isabel would have done better to devote her idealistic energies to a cause, eschewing such wastrels as Osmond and Merle, but merely that she should have charted her course with greater realism and insight.

It may be objected that James neither here nor anywhere else, except in *The Princess Casamassima*, concerned himself with social causes (such as the Zionist cause in *Daniel Deronda*), but the point is that James would have found moral ambiguities wherever he looked. The leisure of his leisured people simply gives them time to ponder their ambiguities.

In James's fiction innocence is destroyed through a failure on the part of one or other of his characters to appreciate its alloyed nature. Thus Winterbourne is circumspect about Daisy Miller, witholding his esteem until it is too late partly because of the possibility that her freedom of manner may contain some taint of calculation and crudity. So, by omission, he bears a slight responsibility for her death by swamp-fever. The governess in 'The Turn of the Screw', whether she suffers from hallucinations or not, kills little Miles chiefly, I suggest, because she cannot reconcile his beauty with his possible wickedness. If the governess is hallucinated, then she is a prime example of the rebellion of the unconscious; if she is not, then some awareness of her affinity with the evil represented by the ghosts, Quint and Jessel, would have saved Miles.

Those of James's characters who most receive the author's sympathy are not good or innocent in a sense that would have satisfied Dickens or George Eliot. In fact James regularly suggests an incompatibility between innocence and adult living, as in the death of Milly Theale in *The Wings of A Dove*. One might go further and say that to James the most comprehensive awareness either is or is the cause of the finest behaviour. Intellectual and moral errors go hand in hand; emotional blindness equals moral infirmity.

James's best or most sympathetic characters adapt themselves to the ways of the world without losing their value. When Catherine Sloper in *Washington Square* finally rises to her full stature she rejects the partially repentant Morris Townsend with a hardness that is wrong by the standards of sentimental ethics (the standards, for example, of Mrs Penniman) but wholly fitting. Maisie Farange in *What Maisie Knew* acquires the stratagems of the selfish adults who surround her while retaining her own capacity to love; Strether in *The Ambassadors* comes to terms with the exploitations practised by Madame de Vionnet and Chad without losing his enthusiasm for Paris, and Maggie Verver in *The Golden Bowl* defeats Amerigo and Charlotte Stant by honourable uses of dishonourable tactics. In all these instances the 'innocent' learns the steps of the dance, the motions of worldliness, but rises above them through a kind of superior awareness that can detect small movements towards addiction.

The way in James is to resist not evil. There is an interesting metaphor in *The Portrait of A Lady* contrasting the 'garden' which is the unsullied soul with 'dusky pestiferous tracts' where many people dwell.[11] One of James's major achievements was to assert that garden and pestiferous tract run into each other, lacking a boundary fence. There is no exact correspondence between the Freudian unconscious and the Jamesian swamp, because the latter is always either known or knowable by the ordinary processes of honest observation. But it is easy to see that some of the selfish or

9

sensual impulses that James's characters have towards one another are of roughly the sort that Freud discovered in his Viennese patients by analysis. Those patients, unlike a great many of James's characters, had a set of fierce canons to live up to and therefore found it necessary to render themselves unaware of libidinal desires.

The nature of the unconscious as depicted by Freud shocked people because the concept seemed to belie, or at least to minimize, man's capacity for reason. But Freud himself was a sort of rationalist who, in holding that man's task was to reclaim for the conscious mind those elements that had been thrust into the unconscious, was simply painting a more realistic picture of man. The implicit theme of Freud's earlier work (the later work is more taken up with the processes of the ego) is to the effect that wild beasts are not necessarily untameable, but you cannot hope to tame them—and are more likely to be destroyed by them—if you do not know that they are there.

This, or something like this, is a central theme in another novelist of our period, Conrad. A closely related theme in Conrad is that if you assume that bestiality is to be found only in less advanced races than your own, races which it is your task to civilize, you may be confounded by the emergence of your own bestiality.

For our present purposes the most interesting feature of Conrad's work is that remarked on by the critic, A. J. Guerard. Conrad, he has asserted, had 'a rationalist's declared distrust of the unconscious and a rationalist's desire to be a sane orderly novelist—doubled by a powerful introspective drive that took the dreamer deeper into the unconscious than any earlier English novelist (except possibly Dickens)'.[12]

It is not that Conrad actually discusses the motives of his characters with reference to unconscious desires, but rather that he dramatizes strange internal conflicts, strange thwartings or reversals of conscious aims. His characters sometimes find themselves co-operating with antagonistic persons or circumstances. Throughout most of the course of *The Nigger of the Narcissus*, for example, James Wait, the 'nigger', is dying from tuberculosis, and his monstrous narcissism brings out the hidden deathliness of his healthy colleagues as their feelings towards him shift about from hatred to pity, from bewilderment to complicity. Wait burrows into the souls of his fellows presumably because his qualities are already lurking there. His disintegration is repulsive, yet disintegration of a sort spreads over the ship, as if the process were so attractive as to invite emulation. Detailed 'Freudian' interpretations of the events of the story are in my opinion undesirable, but one is naturally reminded of Freud's notion of the 'death instincts', which are ego-instincts furthering what Freud called 'the most universal endeavour of all living substance—namely to return to the quiescence of the inorganic world'.[13]

If James Wait's personality draws out concealed elements in the personalities of other characters in the story, how much more plainly is the same principle at work in other novels of Conrad. *Lord Jim*, for instance, is the story of a man who cannot live up to his ego-ideal and finally appears to conclude that morally he has something in common with the brigand, 'Gentleman' Brown.

It will be recalled that Jim, along with fellow officers, jumps overboard from a ship called *Patna*, which is thought to be sinking. His cowardice so dismays him that he stays out East, away from his countrymen, on an island named Patusan where he becomes the venerated leader of the native community. Jim's complete downfall is brought about when a gang of freebooters, headed by 'Gentleman' Brown, comes to Patusan with the vague intention of obtaining spoils. There is a fine scene in which Jim and Brown confront each other across a creek, and Brown, with the insight of a man both highly intelligent and malicious, senses that Jim must have some shameful reason for residing in Patusan. Brown proceeds to insinuate that he and Jim, who both live apart from the societies in which they were reared, are alike in having a guilty past, and it seems (though Conrad is not explicit on this point) that Jim's demoralization and death are the direct results of his accepting Brown's insinuations as the truth.

But to Conrad they are a distorted version of the truth. It is probable that Conrad's own view of the matter is expressed by the words of the Dutch trader, Stein:

A man that is born falls into a dream like a man who falls into the sea. If he tries to climb out into the air as inexperienced people endeavour to do, he drowns—*nicht wahr?* ... No! I tell you! The way is to the destructive element submit yourself, and with the exertions of your hands and feet in the water make the deep, deep sea keep you up.[14]

There are rival interpretations of these celebrated remarks, but the most sensible seems to me to be that of A. J. Guerard, to the effect that man has a dream or ideal of himself to which he should adhere, not by evading the tests of real life (life being the 'destructive element'), but, on the contrary, by submitting himself to such tests and never abandoning the ideal, however often he fails to live up to it.

This way of viewing the relationship between good and evil is perfectly in line with Freudian psychology. Jim's flaw lies in his desire for immaculacy, his assumption that to be worthy of respect

11

he must be virtually different in kind from such a man as Brown. We can judge from Conrad's works that he, like James, saw a need for modern man to accept his own 'dark' side—the darkness of egotism and deathliness as embodied in James Wait, the darkness of malice as represented in Brown—without yielding his high aspirations.

This credo is also apparent in *Heart of Darkness*, in which Conrad's narrator, Marlow, recollects how he was brought up against extremes of savagery and debasement on a journey into the Belgian Congo. Although this story should not, I believe, be read as an allegory, it is impossible for our post-Freudian ears to ignore currents of meaning which flow beyond the Congolese jungle and the decaying phase of European imperialism. The jungle, or most specifically the area of Kurtz's trading station, is not to be equated with the unconscious, but it is a place in which an individual's frail sublimatory structures are liable to break down, exposing him to the onrush of his own primitive impulses. When Marlow remarks of the Thames estuary that 'this also has been one of the dark places of the earth', and when he later states that 'Going up that river [the Congo] was like travelling back to the earliest beginnings of the world', he is making a similar point to Freud's (in the words quoted earlier) that our civilization has been laboriously built up and is insecure. Freud's implication is, as we noted, that the edifice is less likely to crack if we know it is likely to crack, and this is Conrad's message also.

Kurtz, of whom Marlow hears much long before he meets him, has been an extraordinarily efficient trader, a perfect exemplar of European industriousness and enterprise. On coming out to the Congo, Kurtz had compiled a report for the 'International Society for the Suppression of Savage Customs' in which he had argued that 'By the simple exercise of our will we can exert a power for good practically unbounded.' Kurtz's degradation into some sort of perverted sexuality, murder, and (possibly) cannibalism is the consequence of not recognizing his fundamental susceptibility to such activities. The influence of Freud encourages us to see Kurtz's zeal as a trader as the precarious sublimation of sado-masochistic impulses. And the story, as everyone has recognized, is not just about one specific man, but at the least about European man in general, for 'all Europe contributed to the making of Kurtz'.

Conrad further generalizes his meaning by causing Marlow, a balanced and civilized man, to identify himself with Kurtz. It is even possible that the various 'otiose' adjectives ('unspeakable', 'inscrutable', 'monstrous', etc.) with which, to the irritation of some critics, Marlow's narrative is sprinkled, are less the product of feeble artistry than of Conrad's feelings in the face of the underworld of civilized human nature. Lustful murder, for example, is not as such 'unspeakable', but for a prophetic author working in the 1890s a sense of the omnipresent power of what psycho-analysts later called the 'id' or the 'Shadow' might well have justified the use of such a word.

So far in this chapter I have tried to show how the burden of consciousness in the late nineteenth century manifested itself in three novelists of markedly differing temperaments. Broadly speaking the burden took two forms. First there was the philosophical or religious form, the legacy of Darwin and other agents of religious doubt, which can best be expressed as a question: if man is the highest species of life in the universe, how can he relate himself to the rest of nature that envelopes, permeates and controls him? For man's best qualities are rationality and sensitiveness, whereas the rest of nature does not exhibit these qualities, and seems in fact to be hostile to them. This was Hardy's question, posed chiefly through the character of Sue Bridehead. Secondly, the burden took a moral form, consequent upon the growing belief that evil is not only perfectly natural (as opposed to supernatural in its origins) but also indissolubly bound up with good. This is a leading theme in both James and Conrad.

To Freud and other scientifically-minded thinkers, including such writers as Wells and Shaw, the challenge was exhilarating rather than depressing. The way ahead was clear, if tremendously exacting: by exercising his reason man would fulfil his role in the evolutionary process, ultimately (as in Wells's *Men Like Gods* and Shaw's *Back to Methuselah*) producing the next link in the chain. Freud supposed that religion had been a kind of universal neurosis, outgrowing which would bring far greater social and psychological wellbeing. At the close of *The Future of an Illusion* Freud dealt with the religious problem in this way:

In the first place, our organization—that is, our mental apparatus —has been developed precisely in the attempt to explore the external world, and it must therefore have realized in its structure some degree of expediency; in the second place, it is itself a constituent part of the world which we set out to investigate, and it readily admits of such an investigation; thirdly, the task of science is fully covered if we limit it to showing how the world must appear to us in consequence of the particular character of our organization; fourthly, the ultimate findings of science, precisely because of the way in which they are acquired, are determined not only by our organization but by the things which have affected that organization; finally, the problem of the nature of the world without regard to our percipient mental apparatus is an empty abstraction, devoid of practical interest.[15]

The final part of these remarks is logically incontestable, yet to the religious man, in Freud's time or our own, quite unacceptable. Despite the impossibility of grasping the 'nature of the world' except through 'our percipient mental apparatus' (which provides or transmits the mystical vision no less than the chain of reasoning), the religious man feels it impossible to take any step without a notion of ultimate, as opposed to mundane, reality. But this notion is itself a product of his 'percipient mental apparatus'. This absolute crux has frequently—and I think rightly—been assumed to be the pervading theme of Kafka's stories.

The burden of consciousness is heavier in Kafka's works than in the writings of any other author of our period, because he was consistently (though often obliquely) concerned with the very purposes and limitations of consciousness. One of Kafka's aphorisms recorded in his notebooks is as follows:

> Seen with the terrestrially sullied eye, we are in the situation of travellers in a train that has met with an accident in a tunnel, and this at a place where the light of the beginning can no longer be seen, and the light of the end is so very small a glimmer that the gaze must continually search for it and is always losing it again; and furthermore, both the beginning and the end are not even certainties. Round about us, however, in the confusion of our senses, or in the supersensitiveness of our senses, we have nothing but monstrosities and a kaleidoscopic play of things that is either delightful or exhausting. . . . [16]

The opening phrase of this passage, 'seen with the terrestrially sullied eye', asserts that what Freud called 'our percipient mental apparatus' is inadequate, since it cannot discern the meaning of human existence. But why should our vision be sullied? Why cannot we accept the 'expediency' of the mind, as Freud termed it, the evolutionary tendency of consciousness to adapt itself to the demands of its own explorations. Kafka's answer, of course, embodied in the stories and plainly stated in the above aphorism, is that human life is in itself quite senseless: 'nothing but monstrosities and a kaleidoscopic play of things'. This is a fact disguised from most people by their propensity to confer meanings—meanings that would collapse before a moment's honest examination. At the same time it is a faculty of the mind, perhaps indeed its inescapable and sovereign function, to discover or manufacture meaning. Kafka's art was devoted to expressing, in concrete rather than abstract terms, this irreconcilable contradiction.

A reasonable approach to Kafka's tales (though it is only one of many approaches, as a survey of Kafka criticism will show) is to see

them as appalled, though sometimes humorous, responses to Pro-
tagoras's proposition that 'Man is the measure of all things.' If life
is confined to the elements that man himself may comprehend and
qualify then—according to Kafka's view—we have nothing but
absurdity. If a man looked for explainable meaning and purpose in
his daily activities, and especially for some rational link between one
activity and the next, he would see the world as Kafka portrays it.
If he fully accepted that he might pointlessly die the next moment,
that he cannot prove that his actions have any value, that the
patterns he makes of his experiences are at best provisional, that
sequences of cause and effect are more discernible in art than in life,
and that God either does not exist or is totally unknowable, then he
would meet Kafka's stories with a shock of recognition and no itch
to interpret them.

The point of any activity is lost if one asks searchingly enough
what its point is. Nobody can adequately explain (if he subscribes to
as demanding a standard of adequacy as Kafka's) why he wants to
make money, or get married, or read a book: he can say only that
he wants to do such things or that he feels obliged to do them. In
other words, the impulse comes from outside or below the delibera-
tive processes, and the meaning resides in the impulse. The kind of
meaning that the intellect discerns after the impulse has been felt
or the deed done is of a different and less vital nature. But the
heroes of Kafka's novels give priority to this second, less vital sort
of meaning. In this way Joseph K. in *The Trial* needs to know of
what he is guilty before he can get on with the business of living, and
K. in *The Castle* exploits the villagers in order to find out as much as
possible about the Castle. In other words, Joseph K. is in search of
the Law, an extra-human moral order, while K. requires a justification of the entire human order.

Each of these heroes is a lonely *individual* sporadically and more
or less futilely in connection with other people. Their very individuality seems to be both a necessity and a curse: it is, in a sense, their
'crime' that they are cut off from nature and social connections. The
other characters seem to know what they are about but it is clear that
their knowledge is supposed to be a form of self-deception. It is as if
everyone in the two novels except the heroes can accept working
hypotheses, or, alternatively feels able to trust his or her own will.
These 'expedient' procedures are what Kafka himself could not
follow, as is plain not only from the fictions but also from the
biographical material (especially the *Diaries*, the *Letter to His
Father* and the *Letters to Felice*). Kakfa had little will in the ordinary
affairs of life but fanatical will in relation to his writing. All his will,
in other words, went into expressing a will-less vision. There was an
absolute refusal to sweep away the objections of his critical intell-

igence so that little could be decisively done merely from personal desire. His project was to deny the validity of all projects. Accordingly Joseph K. and K. are both dogged characters (K. is even aggressive); but dogged in their reluctance to beg fundamental questions. Thus, just before his execution Joseph K. tells himself that 'the only thing for me to do is to keep my intelligence cold and analytic to the end'. He does not know what he wants, because he cannot discover what he should want. This is not will in the ordinary sense, but a resolute denial of personal will. Similarly, K. employs a variety of means—cajoling, hectoring, straightforward enquiry and so on—not just in order to stay with the barmaid, Frieda, for example, or to be allowed to remain in the schoolroom, but only to get into the Castle or otherwise apprehend its nature. In Kafka the provisional is dependent on the ultimate, and since the ultimate is shrouded in mystery, the provisional either is plainly ridiculous, or, perhaps just occasionally, contains a glimmer of real meaning.

So Kafka's novels and stories bring rationalism and the religious spirit into sharpest conflict. From this standpoint the rationalist eats his cake and has it, because he enthrones reason and then burkes the very problems that so resplendent a faculty should be directed towards solving. But to the rationalist who takes an evolutionary view the religious problem is simply an encumbrance left over from centuries of monotheism. It is strictly a non-problem, except in the sense of an anthropological phenomenon now ripe for analysis.

This, as we have noted, was how Freud saw the matter. Freud took the commonsensical view that the mystery of existence itself must be left aside while reason devotes itself to answerable questions. Man differs from the lower animals not in having an immortal soul but in having a larger brain, so that he can ponder his own nature; whereas the chimpanzee, for instance, can solve only elementary problems. But man is yet an animal who in Freud's opinion, expressed in *Totem and Taboo*, has passed through three systems of thought, 'three great pictures of the universe: animistic (or mythological), religious and scientific.'[17] The last is not greater than the first two (and it is certainly less comprehensive), but it is our *present* system of thought, though we retain traces of animism and large elements of religion. It is presumably (though Freud did not explicitly say so) these relics of former systems that make men such as Kafka cry out for absolute explanation. Freud had no doubt that such an attitude is morbid: 'He who asks what is the meaning of life is already sick. The meaning of life is life itself.'

In relation to our theme Freud's task was twofold: first to convince his readers of their inherent irrationalities, the animalistic foundations of their human nature; and secondly to assign reason to its

16

true place. In the Freudian scheme reason is not a godlike faculty, nor is-it exactly a kind of warder of the instincts, but primarily an ego-faculty whose purpose is to relate instinctual impulses to their possibilities of satisfaction in the social world. However, it is fair to judge from the tenor of Freud's entire work that he believed that reason could, as a result of acknowledging its humble role in relation to the instincts, sooner or later become the guiding faculty that it had for so long merely (and disastrously) pretended to be. The last novelist I shall deal with in this chapter, Thomas Mann, who wrestled more explicitly with the burden of consciousness than any other author of the time, and who was deeply influenced by Freud, recognized this important feature of Freud's work.

Mann's essay, 'Freud's Position in the History of Modern Thought' (1930), places Freud in an intellectual tradition, in regard to the enlightened use of the forces of irrationality. Freud's work, Mann insists, can be called anti-rational only with reference to its subject-matter: its object, however, is to transcend the irrational. Mann concludes the essay as follows:

It [Freud's teaching] might be called anti-rational, since it deals, in the interests of research, with the night, the dream, impulse, the pre-rational; and the concept of the unconscious presides at its beginnings. But it is far from letting those interests make it a tool of the obscurantist, fanatic, backward-shaping spirit. It is that manifestation of modern irrationalism which stands un-equivocally firm against all reactionary misuse. It is, to my sincere conviction, one of the great foundation-stones to a structure of the future which shall be the dwelling-place of a free and conscious humanity.[18]

Mann's enthusiasm for Freud's approach to the age-old problem of passion versus reason was due to certain explorations of his own that had led him in the same direction. To begin with, for obvious biographical reasons, Mann was concerned with the rival claims of the bourgeois way of life and that of the artist, but these alternatives were merely the first form in which Mann encountered a much wider-ranging antinomy. Something similar to Mann's beginnings is apparent in Galsworthy's *The Forsyte Saga* and in E. M. Forster's faintly Germanic novel, *Howards End*. Mann, like Galsworthy and Forster, was impressed by the cleavage between the life devoted to beauty and art and the life given over to action and utility, the former being understood to depend on a respect for the emotions, the latter on an allegiance to social forms. Mann—again like Galsworthy and Forster—could not plump unreservedly for the first way, despite his artist's nature, since he saw in it certain social deficiencies. Just as Galsworthy produced a far more convincing and robust picture of his arch-bourgeois, Soames Forsyte, than he did of his 'artists', such as Irene and Young Jolyon, and rather as Forster reserved some credit for his unimaginative businessman Henry Wilcox, as well as for his representative of sensibility, Helen Schlegel, so also Mann tried to accommodate the two attitudes to life. In *Buddenbrooks*, Mann's first full-length novel, the Buddenbrook line begins so far as the story is concerned with Johann, a prosperous, worldly *bürger*, and ends with the musically talented but sickly boy, Hanno, who dies at the time the family business goes into liquidation. Young Hanno is not preferable to old Johann: the two characters are just extreme representatives of what Mann then saw as irreconcilable sets of values. Similarly, *Tonio Kröger*, another novel of Mann's early period, is a dramatized rumination on the relationship between the poetic and the practical natures. The reader follows Tonio, the son of a sternly successful father and a beautifully latinate mother, from his indolent schooldays to his young manhood. Tonio, who has consistently felt himself to be unworthy by extrovert middle-class standards, concludes in a letter to a discerning Russian friend, Lisabeta Ivanovna, that he is a '*bourgeois* who strayed off into art, a bohemian who feels nostalgic yearnings for respectability, an artist with a bad conscience'. The explicit contrast is between full-hearted engagement with life and knowledge of life, as if the two were necessarily incompatible. But built into this slight story is the groundwork of Mann's solution of the problem, for Tonio states that 'if anything is capable of making a poet of a literary man, it is my *bourgeois* love of the human, the living and usual'. (One thinks of how another young artist of this period, Joyce's Stephen Dedalus, passes from an awareness, in *A Portrait of the Artist as a Young Man*, that he is cut off from the simple joys experienced by his father to achieving rapport with Bloom and, by implication, with Molly towards the end of *Ulysses*.)

In Mann's work at least up to the time of *The Magic Mountain* 1924), and prominently including *Death in Venice* (1911), there is the regular portrayal of an opposition between knowledge of a particular kind and sane, vigorous living. Such knowledge is associated with disease and death: it belongs to 'spirit' rather than to 'nature', and for this reason subverts both joy and bodily health. The knowledge of Gustave von Aschenbach, for example, in *Death in Venice* is a by-product of a will aimed steadily from his precocious boyhood onwards to the attainment of literary and intellectual eminence; yet we learn that one of Aschenbach's highly-praised stories dealt with the means by which will or 'moral fibre' can conquer ennervating knowledge. It seems indeed that Aschenbach's disintegration is the result of a failure to understand that knowledge and will, as he has understood these qualities, far from being hostile to each other, are in secret alliance against 'nature'.

Aschenbach is presumably intended to be a greatly admired rather than a great writer, for, apart from anything else, the faintly spurious formality and fastidiousness of the style of the story seems to reflect the mind of its hero. In Mann's view, however, as expressed in such essays as 'Goethe and Tolstoy' and 'Tolstoy', genuinely great writers can be creatures of spirit as opposed to nature. Mann's version of the essential difference between Dostoevsky and Tolstoy is that the former exhibited nobility of spirit, the latter nobility of nature. It is clear what Mann means by 'spirit': he refers to the aspiration to escape from biological restrictions. Conversely, the other kind of writer—Tolstoy or Goethe—is at home with natural phenomena. 'Spirit', writes Mann, 'is that which distinguishes from all other forms of organic life this creature man, this being which is to such a high degree independent of her and hostile to her.'[19] Tolstoy, on the other hand, was a healthy 'child of nature' whose forays into the territory of spirit were clumsy in the extreme.

It is easy to grasp and accept the sort of distinction Mann made, even as a number of objections rise up against the distinction. Mann himself wrestled with many qualifying factors and seemed to conclude that life is an interplay or oscillation between the poles of spirit and nature: if the writer belongs mainly to one category he may at least venture sporadically in the direction of the other. The writer who is basically a child of nature accepts the world and is on the whole willing to subordinate himself to objective realities. He values health, vitality, the senses, the instincts. His knowledge is generally knowledge of concrete and material realities, or of ideas that do not seek to controvert such realities. His emotions, titanic or trivial, are regarded as phenomena, rather than as arbiters of the universe. Such a writer is not necessarily 'objective' in the narrow sense: the category would presumably include both the highly subjective Virginia Woolf and the objective Arnold Bennett, but it would exclude Hardy and Kafka, both of whom (in their otherwise wholly dissimilar ways) yearned to defy earthly conditions.

On the other hand, the writer of strong spiritual leanings—say Dostoevsky or Schiller—cannot accept life as meaningful in so far as he is governed by biological laws. This is not in a limited sense a moral matter—Dostoevsky's Stavrogin or his Ivan Karamazov is as immoral as his Prince Myshkin or his Father Zossima is moral. To such characters, as to their creator, health and even life itself are not paramount: only the yearning for a higher—that is, a freer—mode of existence really matters.

Mann himself never asserted that one class of writer (or one attitude to life) is preferable to the other: despite his reverence for

19

Goethe and Tolstoy, both 'children of nature', he continued to value the explorations of more spiritual men. *The Magic Mountain*, for example, explicitly sets exponents of the two attitudes against each other, and while one of them wins the day, his triumph requires interpretation. The hero, Hans Castorp, staying at the Berghof Sanatorium at Davos, is for a long time fascinated by the rival arguments and personalities of two men, the first an Italian humanist called Settembrini to whom the irrational (including the mystical) is not merely bad but deathly; and the second a Jesuitical communist named Naphta who favours indifference to the affairs of this world and, when politically 'necessary', judicial murder. Both disputants talk of 'spirit', but Settembrini (who can be tiresome and, for all his cleverness, rather absurd) has in mind the disinterested search for truth, while Naphta (who is ugly, formidable and perhaps an exposer of shallownesses) means that which stands completely apart from life and the ordinary processes of mind. Settembrini is an agressive monist; Naphta, a confirmed dualist. In the section entitled 'Hysterica Passio' these two disputants have a duel: Settembrini bravely fires his pistol into the air and then Naphta shoots himself in the head. Mann's implication is that Naphta has all along been in love with death, a truly regressive character, while Settembrini has a healthy will. But the will of such progressivists as Settembrini needs to be informed by a subtle understanding of the Naphta components of human nature.

In the penultimate chapter of the novel, in the section entitled 'Snow', Hans Castorp, by now tired of the arguments of Naphta and Settembrini, sets off to ski in the mountains, but loses his way in a snowstorm and falls asleep beside a mountain hut. He dreams of an arcadian scene, a Mediterranean shore of surpassing beauty on which are a number of serene, loving and handsome people. Back from the shore, however, is a temple inside which, as Hans discovers when he enters, are two witchlike women dismembering and eating a child. But it seems to Hans when the dream is over that the happy people on the shore were aware of, and accepted, the atrocious activities in the temple. He concludes that Naphta and Settembrini are both wrong, for 'Man is the lord of counter-positions', and therefore should not occupy a partial standpoint. In the postscript to the English edition of *The Magic Mountain* Mann writes that Hans Castorp should probably be regarded as a Quester for the Holy Grail and the Grail itself be understood, on the lines of the 'Snow' dream, as 'the conception of a future humanity that has passed through and survived the profoundest knowledge of disease and death'.[20] In this way Mann hoped to make a contribution, not altogether unlike Freud's, towards uniting reason with the irrational, the Apollonian with the Dionysian, the conscious and civilized with the most primitive and barbaric.

We should move out of our immediate period if we gave much attention to Mann's later works, but it should be said that as late as 1947, when *Dr Faustus* appeared, Mann presented a hero who seeks spiritual grandeur through a career of sin. Mann's Faustian composer, Adrian Leverkühn, unlike Marlowe's Faustus or Goethe's Faust, believes that a life deliberately given over to the devil will actually enhance his prospects of salvation—provided he can make a final act of contrition. The ruffianly devil who appears before Leverkühn counters Leverkühn's casuistries with more effective ones, but argues rightly that the composer will have become incapable of contrition when his time is up. What the devil candidly offers is a period of heightened genius indissolubly linked with moral and physical infirmity. In other words, some great human productions—such as Leverkühn's compositions—that soar towards the spiritual heights owe their existence to barbaric and morbid elements in man. They, or their creators, pass through 'the profoundest knowledge of disease and death'.

In between *The Magic Mountain* and *Dr Faustus* the most revealing story for our purposes is *Mario and the Magician* (though it is worth pointing out in passing that the Joseph novels present a God who unites within Himself the principles of Good and Evil, the most perfect moral consciousness and the most abundant non-moral vitality). *Mario and the Magician* deals with the distinction between the conscious and the unconscious will. The hunchbacked hypnotist, Cipolla, gives an exhibition of his powers in a hall in a small Italian seaside town. Among the fascinated but barely comprehending audience is the German narrator, together with his family. Cipolla is eloquently arrogant and provocative: his remarks are a kind of performance in themselves. He insults the audience so that some people are moved to answer him back. He does some ordinary— though still mysterious—tricks with cards and numbers, but the remarkable feature of his act is his capacity for causing members of the audience to do things against their wills. He successfully orders one young man to stick his tongue out and later to double up as if with stomach pains. After that a man of soldierly bearing finds himself unable to raise his arm. It is not that these particular individuals are put into a trance (though other individuals are): they simply yield to Cipolla's will. Finally a young waiter called Mario, known to the narrator and his family, is caused to kiss the hunchback's cheek precisely as though he were kissing his girl, Silvestra. But after stumbling in humiliation off the stage, Mario turns and shoots the hypnotist dead.

The story has often been seen as a commentary on the power of Mussolini and his fascists, but it has wider implications. The hypnotist states to his audience: 'Freedom exists, and also the will exists; but freedom of the will does not exist, for a will that aims at its own freedom aims at the unknown.' In the light of the whole story this remark appears to mean that one cannot choose what to will, since the will is primary. The will must have an object; that is one must will *something* (some end, some course of action), but this something can be known only after one has willed it. Therefore, he who tries to make his will free, in other words subject to rational pre-determination, 'aims at the unknown'. Cipolla, whose name is the Italian for onion, is presumably a many-layered creature without a core of personal hopes, fears, attachments, beliefs: he is a pure servant of the will, who in any situation desires only a meaningless ascendancy over others. Other people in fact submit to him (or rather to his will, for he is nothing 'in himself') because they do possess a core and because their wills at the time are merely negative.

The relevance of this story to our theme is that Mann, like Freud, was profoundly interested in the non-rational basis of our desires. The outcome of the events is willed by both Mario and Cipolla, but it is not rationally willed. Mario's will to shoot is spontaneous, surprising himself as much as anyone else; while Cipolla perhaps was always aiming at his own destruction, always 'asking for it'. In neither case, however, was the desire rational. Similarly, the will of Aschenbach in *Death in Venice* directs him, quite without conscious design, to Venice, to the beautiful boy, Tadzio, and to his own death.

Aschenbach, the dignified, orderly writer, and Cipolla, the demoniac hypnotist, appear to stand at opposite poles from each other, but they are alike in being possessed by an impulse to disintegration. The former has sought, up to the point in his life at which *Death in Venice* begins, to control his own destiny by arduous intellectual work marked by control and formality. He has seemed to be an apostle of reason, but he has underestimated the power of the irrational forces in his own nature. Cipolla, on the other hand, has made himself into an agent of irrational forces, perhaps in the awareness that sooner or later he will be destroyed by them.

These two characters perfectly represent what Mann saw as a dangerous element in German culture, an antidote to which was at last being provided by Freud. In the essay on Freud Mann also declares himself in favour of the 'revolutionary principle'.

The revolutionary principle is simply the will towards the future, which Novalis called 'the really better world'. It is the principle of consciousness and recognition, leading to higher levels; the will and the urge to destroy—by means of lifting them into con-

22

sciousness—all the premature apparent harmonies and pseudo-perfections of life, that rest upon certain and morally inadequate awareness; and by analysis, by psychology, through phases of solution, which from the point of view of cultural unity, must be designated as anarchy, but in which there is no pause and no retreat, no restoration, no tenable standing ground, to break a path to a free and genuine unity of existence, secured by conscious possession, to the culture of men developed to complete self-consciousness.[21]

The dangerous element that Mann analyses in this essay had two faces, well represented by Aschenbach and Cipolla. The first face evinced satisfaction with 'all the premature apparent harmonies and pseudo-perfections of life'; it sought to ignore the anarchy within, or else to abolish the anarchy, as if by decree. This tendency was utterly unrealistic, though it was not necessarily ignoble. It is represented on one level by Aschenbach's theme of 'aristocratic self-command'; on another level—to pass beyond Mann's own works—it is illustrated by the crude attempts of Conrad's Kurtz to suppress savage customs. Indeed, in the widest sense, any impatience with man's amphibious make-up resulting in disdain for the instincts is part of the danger. The other part, the other face, is positively ignoble, for it welcomes barbarism. The tendency here is to sink into anarchy, as Aschenbach does towards the end of his life, or as Kurtz comes to participate in the savage customs that he formerly worked to suppress.

Freud's solution, as Mann saw it, was to acknowledge the anarchy within, but not to surrender to it. In this way the forces of 'reaction' could be enlisted in the service of revolution; residual elements of even the most primeval impulses could be used to aid the march towards greater consciousness and freedom.

2

THE NATURE OF THE UNCONSCIOUS

Freud, Joyce and Lawrence

As we have seen in the preceding chapter, Thomas Mann regarded Freud's work as reactionary in subject-matter but revolutionary in direction: Freud was delving backwards in order to move forwards; he was acknowledging the irrational for the purpose of promoting rationality. The assumption behind this view of Freud was that progress in human affairs consists of increase in consciousness, which means also increase in freedom. In Mann's eyes Freud's work was 'one of the great foundation-stones to a structure of the future which shall be the dwelling-place of a free and conscious humanity'. Creatures—so the implicit argument runs—are the less free the less they understand the forces that move them. So a human being is much more free than a lower animal, and a modern man, especially a man such as Freud, who has undertaken a profound course of self-analysis, is freer than a primitive.

No doubt many people find this strand of evolutionistic thinking unexceptionable, and indeed obvious, but I wish in this chapter to examine a contrast between the Freudian version of the unconscious and a rival, literary version that is involved with different notions of human progress and values. It is necessary first to look in some detail at what Freud meant by the unconscious, because his meaning is still commonly misrepresented.

Freud began his work in the field of neurology, but in the 1880s, mainly as the result of contacts with Breuer and Charcot, he came to believe that nervous disorders were more amenable to comprehension and cure through psychological investigation than through the study of the nervous system. Just the same, a physiological hypothesis underlies Freud's psychological concept of the unconscious. In brief, according to this hypothesis the human body is like a tank or reservoir containing a fixed amount of excitation, which Freud called 'Quantity'. Quantity is produced either by external factors (what the senses perceive) or by internal instincts, and it is discharged by the various forms of expressive behaviour, but the sum total of Quantity in the body remains constant. The nervous system consists of nerve-fibres connecting nerve-cells or 'neurones', and each neurone acts to expel Quantity along the fibres to the next neurone. The whole notion really is best understood on the analogy of a water-tank, with an inlet and an outlet pipe, except for the complication that some 'water' is actually manufactured within the tank. The water is propelled from one point to the next along a great complex of internal pipes. However, there is in the body a special organization of neurones called the 'ego', and this organization usually acts to impede the flow. The function of the ego is to enable the person to distinguish between the outer world and the inner, to know which part of whatever is exciting him is an external event and which part is an instinctual impulse. In hallucination, which occurs when the ego is weak or malfunctioning, the person 'sees' (or 'hears' etc.) an object in the external world that is really only the image-manifestation of an instinctual impulse. If there were no ego we should be constantly hallucinated and therefore quite incompetent.

When there is unimpeded flow from neurone to neurone, because the ego realizes that external circumstances are propitious, the nervous system is undergoing what Freud called the 'Primary Processes', and the feeling experienced is 'Pleasure'; when the ego checks the flow, the nervous system is undergoing the 'Secondary Processes', and the feeling experienced is 'Pain', that is, unpleasure. Human beings naturally seek 'Pleasure', or, in other words, they seek to live perpetually without any damming up of instinctual desires. But the Primary Processes are—or are 'in'—the unconscious, so the human being desires to live unconsciously, like an animal or an infant, or in accordance with the myth of Adam and Eve before the Fall. The demands of reality, of the external world, prevent this most of the time, and so enable us to produce the works of civilization. Even ordinary thoughts are a consequence of the Secondary Processes, that is, of unpleasure.

The Primary Processes are the activity of the unconscious, unknowable except by inference. An instinct cannot be directly known; it can be experienced only as an idea or an emotion, but such ideas and emotions are not the instincts themselves. The unconscious is quite out of touch with the realities of life, completely senseless. It is a riot of instincts that can contradict one another in their demands and have no awareness of danger or of time. In a metapsychological essay of 1915, 'The Unconscious', Freud wrote that the characteristics of the unconscious are 'exemption from mutual contradiction, primary process (motility of cathexis), timelessness, and substitution of psychic for external reality.'[1]

Freud's concept of the unconscious was not arrived at once and for all at a comparatively early stage in his career. He seems to have begun by believing that the unconscious was the repository of material repressed from consciousness, then moved to a phase of believing that some material is originally unconscious, then finally considered that in earliest infancy everything is unconscious. This later view (which, as we shall see, is like Jung's in one respect) was to the effect that the baby progressively passes from unconsciousness to some degree of consciousness. To begin with he is all Primary Process, having next to no awareness of the compulsions of the real world. Bit by bit these compulsions force some of the contents of the baby's mind into consciousness or into the preconscious, that is the 'area' of the mind that is susceptible to full awareness under everyday conditions. The preconscious consists of mental activities that at any given moment lie outside the focus of attention but it includes some discomforting or inconvenient thoughts from which the individual shies away. There is a sharp division between the unconscious and the preconscious though the allocation of an 'idea' to one or the other depends upon the degree of resistance to be overcome for the idea to emerge into consciousness. Elements of the unconscious proper present themselves only in disguised forms and are extraordinarily difficult to unmask. For this reason novelists are commonly concerned with the ego rather than the id, even if some of the ego-processes are unrecognized by the fictional characters or are recognized in moments of self-discovery. Lawrence and Joyce, whom I shall be discussing later in this chapter, are two of the very few novelists who deliberately try to represent in some fashion the unconscious itself.

At this stage we come to an aspect of Freud's thought that is more familiar to literary people and to laymen generally—the notion of repression. We have already seen that the ego in Freudian terminology is an organization that mediates between instinctual desires and the external world. The result is an inhibition of the desires, a channelling of them into permissible and socially useful activities, and this is a constant and normal process in human beings. Repression, however, is a different matter. In represssion an emotionally-charged idea is pushed out of consciousness because its presence in consciousness causes great pain. An 'idea' in this sense is not an intellectual idea; it is not an abstraction or a proposition; it is, on the contrary, a completely subjective thought or attitude. Thus a small girl may be afraid of her mother and this response to the mother, highly particularized in respect of actual moments in the girl's life, constitutes an 'idea' in Freud's terms. Such an idea is liable to be repressed because it conflicts with the child's notion of what she feels towards her mother, and, having been repressed, may sooner or later give rise to one or other of the symptoms of neurosis. The mechanism of the neurosis is that the emotion (in this instance fear) is split away from the object, the mother, and attached to some other object that happens to be associated in the child's mind with the mother, though the child is not aware of this association.

Psycho-analysis proceeds by uncovering repressed material. That is to say that the child, now perhaps an adult, is relieved of her symptoms by becoming aware of her fear of her mother, who has perhaps been dead for many years. It is not enough that the patient comes to appreciate the general idea, 'I fear my mother', for she needs to re-admit to consciousness her specific 'idea', which will consist of buried memories. She will also experience again ('abreact') the childhood feelings.

Such in outline is the main batch of elements of Freudian theory germane to our present purpose. Something must now be added about the nature of dreams. It is here of course that the symbolism adduced or discovered by the psycho-analysts, and at one time so fascinating to literary critics, looms up. But I am much less concerned with such matters as the interpretation of sticks, swords, towers and the like as images of the penis than with more fundamental issues. Freud wrote that 'The interpretation of dreams is the royal road to a knowledge of the unconscious activities of the mind',[2] meaning that in examining dreams we can observe the unconscious at work rather than merely drawing inferences from people's words and behaviour. Freud believed that dreams generally express wishes, or, to be more exact, they enact the fulfilment of wishes. More precisely still, dreams are expressions of the Primary Processes, taking their rise from an ego-less realm in which there are no such things as wishes, because there are no impediments.

It has always been difficult to understand why dreams enact wishes as many dreams are of unpleasant happenings, and surely no one actually wants, for instance, to be pursued by a madman brandishing an axe. Nor is it enough to remark that the madman and his axe are merely symbolic, for whatever they are symbolic of must also be frightening. Freud's answer was to the effect that there really is a wish to be overwhelmed by the madman (who is perhaps the dreamer's own aggressive sexuality), though this wish is experienced as fear because it conflicts with other, more righteous wishes.[3]

As is well known, Freud divided the material of dreams into 'Manifest Content' and 'Latent Content'. The Manifest Content is what we experience in the dream, or, at all events, what on waking we remember having experienced. The Latent Content is the underlying meaning, the reality to which the things in the dream give (often bizarre) clues. The dream is like a picture puzzle containing a number of ill-assorted objects. Each object stands for something else, and when every clue has been teased out the picture gives a coherent message. Alternatively the dream is like a charade, each dramatic act of which can be made to yield up part of the total word or phrase. The disguises or clues in a dream are manufactured in three separable but sometimes combined ways called 'Condensation', 'Displacement', and 'Representation'. Condensation means the process by which a number of meanings are fused into one dream-image, rather as literary symbols often represent a mixture of emotions and ideas. Displacement refers to two dream-mechanisms. The first of these is manifested in the tendency of dreams to be misleading about the relative significance of their components. Thus the fact that the madman is wielding the axe may be no more significant than the apparently trivial fact of his wearing a grey coat. In this way emphasis in dreams is 'displaced' according to the standard of wakefulness. By Displacement Freud also meant the occurrence in a dream of some image or word which on analysis is found to act as a link between ideas associated in the dreamer's mind. Representation, the third process of dreams, refers simply but comprehensively to the entire business of transposing thoughts into images.

With the summary of some leading Freudian concepts in mind we can proceed to the examination of a novelistic parallel, namely the 'Circe' episode in Joyce's *Ulysses*. Curiously enough, it is Joyce alone of all the major novelists of this century whose work at times has the true Freudian flavour. Obviously there are many other writers of all periods whose works are highly susceptible to Freud's type of analysis and there are modern writers who have included psycho-analytical ideas in their stories, but generally speaking creative writers wish to foster precisely the sort of values that psycho-analysis is thought to demean. It has often been said that Freud's work was 'reductive' in the sense that it reduced the myriad activities of the psyche to sexual fundamentals and in so doing belittled social, cultural and religious values. It is not necessary to share this view of Freud's work in order to understand why few serious novelists would sense fruitful possibilities in working along strict Freudian lines. Freud neither professionally interested himself in the minutiae of individual differences nor (in contrast to Jung) tried to erect a value-system for post-Christian man. Therefore to follow Freud faithfully (or independently to pursue similar paths) would seem on the face of it to be a method of negating one's aims as a novelist.

But Joyce succeeded in 'reducing' his hero, Leopold Bloom, without diminishing him in our eyes. At first sight amid the excitement and bewilderment over *Ulysses* in the early 1920s, this was not always apparent. I have in mind not just ordinarily uncomprehending or philistine responses but that Jung on reading *Ulysses* was appalled. Jung's essay on *Ulysses* is unintentionally instructive for it reveals the immense difference between his approach to psychology and Freud's. Jung devotes almost the entire essay to desperate assertions that human life is not as Joyce portrays it to be, and then on the final page swings round to the conjecture that Joyce may be right after all. Joyce might have a truly superior mind that can cut through the welter of delusions by which we live; but if so how are we to cope with this new knowledge of ourselves?[4]

Joyce, however, saw Bloom as a good man: he told Frank Budgen that he intended his Ulysses to be a 'complete man' and a 'good man'.[5] Bloom is better than any other leading character in the novel, including Stephen Dedalus himself. In other words Joyce managed to portray the sordid fundamentals of Bloom's personality while preserving Bloom's moral value. It is safe to assume that if the unconscious of such an odious character as Blazes Boylan had been similarly exposed the degree (though not the precise nature) of the sordidness would have been the same. But Bloom is good and Boylan is bad, because morality lies in the transmutation of the underlying processes—alloyed gold out of dross, comparatively pure material out of original slime. This is exactly how Freud saw the moral question.

At the beginning of the fifteenth episode of *Ulysses*, 'Circe', Bloom pursues Stephen and Stephen's friend, Lynch, into Nighttown, the brothel quarter of Dublin: at the conclusion of the episode Bloom is protectively standing over Stephen, who has been knocked to the ground in an argument with an English soldier. This section of the novel parallels the part of the *Odyssey* in which Ulysses' men are drugged and magically turned into swine at Circe's palace. Ulysses himself, who comes after his men to rescue them, is able to overcome Circe because Hermes has given him a magic potion that immunizes him against all Circe's methods of enchantment. Joyce's notion of a modern equivalent to the turning of men into swine is the surrender of men to their bestial impulses. 'Circe' is an episode of dirt, degradation, deformity, lasciviousness; of the body, one might say, divorced from soul. Bloom, however, the Ulysses of the novel, remains unenchanted since his overriding concern throughout the proceedings is for the protection of Stephen and the consequent (but as yet very dimly foreseen) acquisition of a spiritual son.

In his behaviour, therefore, Bloom is comparatively sensible, alert, sober; but the underside of his character is nevertheless revealed. He seems to experience what critics have commonly called 'hallucinations', though it is obvious that they are not proper hallucinations, since Bloom is in a fairly stable frame of mind, capable of conducting normal activities, and the visions ascribed to him are too elaborate. In fact for the most part he does not experience these visions or fantasies at all; Joyce simply invented a stylized technique for portraying what Bloom would experience if he somehow allowed the contents of his unconscious to seep through into his conscious reflections. The visions have something of the quality of waking dreams (not daydreams), except that their meaning is too clear. One has to imagine that material having some of the qualities of a dream (arbitrariness, absurdity) comes floating into Bloom's mind without in the least impairing his faculties. In one sense Joyce's technique is anything but realistic; in another sense, if one accepts the postulates of psycho-analysis, it is a technique for laying bare the real.

As Bloom rather wearily (in a state of 'brainfogfag') wanders through the streets of Nighttown he sees various personages and engages in conversations with them, varying from brief exchanges to a species of trial in which Bloom is the defendant. As I have said, we are not necessarily or invariably to suppose that Bloom receives images of these people but for convenience I will speak as though he does. It is possible, for instance, that to begin with he does imagine the presence of a sinister figure in a sombrero leaning against a wall, a 'Gothic league spy' sent by the Citizen, the aggressive Irish nationalist with whom Bloom has had a row earlier in the evening. However we are not to believe that immediately afterwards Bloom has fantasy conversations with his dead father and his absent wife. Nevertheless old Rudolf Virag appears (he changed his name to Bloom) not exactly as he was in life but with accoutrements that sum up his significance now in the mind of his son; for example, the caftan of an elder of Zion, and streaks of poison upon his face, connoting his suicide. Bloom feels guilty over his backsliding, so the ultra-Jewish vision of Bloom's mother, Ellen, also appears and adds to the scolding. Next comes Molly Bloom, beautiful and contemptuous in Turkish costume. She is superior, sensual, inaccessible (because of a yashmak) and bears a coin on her forehead. Flustered, Bloom says to her: 'I can give you . . . I mean as your business menagerer . . . Mrs Marion . . . if . . .'

Here is something very like a dream, displaying the processes of Condensation, Displacement and Representation, and giving us insights into Bloom that he himself does not possess. Of course the tenor of the vision is clear enough and could not be otherwise, for Joyce is not out to puzzle us unduly. It is true also that if Bloom 'really' experienced the fantasy, he would know what to make of most of it, but even this relative transparency is not un-Freudian, for *The Interpretation of Dreams* does not maintain (in contradiction of common experience) that all dreams are heavily disguised.

Molly's eastern dress, which in itself suggests only the crude stereotype of the lush and yielding slave-girl ('her ankles are linked by a slender fetterchain'), is qualified by her condescending manner. Bloom feels that he ought to desire her aggressively but in fact he is submissive, compliant, slave of a slave. The yashmak holds off not other men but Bloom, her husband, because he has been impotent since the death of their son. The coin on Molly's brow represents the money that Molly may have received that afternoon from Blazes Boylan, her lover and so-called business manager. When Bloom speaks to her he tries to assume some influence over her by announcing himself as her manager, but he addresses her deferentially as 'Mrs Marion'. The word 'manager' comes out as 'menagerer' embracing the ideas of ménage (Bloom's house has become an illicit love nest) and menagerie. The portmanteau word is both quintessentially Joycean (the norm of *Finnegans Wake*) and an example of Displacement, similar to the actual example (the word 'propyl') that Freud produces in *The Interpretation of Dreams*.[6]

The bulk of 'Circe' is on the lines of this small sample, though vastly more complicated than I have indicated. The episode is a phantasmagoric meeting-place of many of the themes, incidents and personalities of the novel. It is very funny, both in pure ribaldry and in satire. The narrative of Bloom's pursuit and custodianship of Stephen moves forward unobtrusively amid the far greater quantity of fantasy material. But it is Bloom alone of all the medley of personalities of whom our knowledge is deepened. It is not that we see him in a fresh light, but that the substratum of his outward personality and his habitual ways of thinking is uncovered. This chiefly happens in the 'trial'.

Shortly after the vision of Molly, two policemen (who are no more present than Molly) question Bloom suspiciously. In a rambling reply Bloom talks of 'circus life', which phrase brings into the scene Signor Maffei, a lion-tamer from the novelette that Molly is currently reading. The 'monster Maffei' carries a hoop, a carriage-whip and a revolver, and against this virile and sadistic figure Bloom begins to put up the 'defence' that he is an honourable professional man, a dentist. On being further questioned by the watch Bloom affects a man-of-the world manner, which is shortly deflated by the appearance of Martha, the typist with whom Bloom is carrying on a tepid romance by correspondence. She (wearing a crimson halter round her neck) accuses him of breach of promise, at which point, Bloom begins to address the assembly as 'Gentlemen of the jury'. Initially his defence is that he is well-connected—with gallant soldiers and policemen—and furthermore that he is an 'author-journalist'. This latest pretension is punctured by the apparition of Philip Beaufoy, the winner of a short-story competition, who in drawling upper-class tones informs everyone that Bloom hasn't even been to a university. Beaufoy's denunciations of Bloom as a 'low cad' are interrupted by the arrival of Mary Driscoll, a scullery-maid who once worked in the Bloom household and who now recounts her (truthful) tale of how Bloom years before mildly assaulted her 'in the rere of the premises'. In response the accused delivers an incoherent statement about his desire to spend the autumn of his life in the bosom of his family. Bloom sometimes turns into whatever he is alleged to be. For instance, when the advocate, O'Molloy, offers the defence that Bloom is 'of Mongolian extraction and irresponsible for his actions', Bloom promptly becomes a Mongol, an idiot. Mainly though, Bloom's varying pleas have to do with his superior social status. When he claims to know the Viceroy of Ireland there appear in turn three society ladies who allege that Bloom has made improper advances to them. Mrs Yelverton Barry, Mrs Bellingham and the Honourable Mrs Mervyn Talboys are typical figures from the old gossip-columns or turn-of-the-century pornography. The last of the three, amazonian and jack-booted, says that she will 'scourge the pigeonlivered cur', this being in excessive response to Bloom's request to be whipped by her. And so, as the accusations mount from all sides (Bloom is said to be every kind of criminal from Jack the Ripper to a 'well-known dynamitard') preparations begin for his hanging. But at about this point Bloom 'actually' encounters Zoe Higgins, the prostitute, who tells him where to find Stephen.

These proceedings are not mainly an illustration of Bloom's unconscious at work—in the full Freudian sense—but rather an uninterrupted flow from the hinterlands of the unconscious up through the preconscious to the conscious mind of the hero. The three systems, Ucs, Pcs, and Cs, as Freud denominated them, are all on display at once. In other words, some features of the fantasy-trial are such that Bloom would on a normal day be hazily aware of them: others, from the preconscious, are such that if Bloom were apprised of them he would not be amazed, while others, from at least the outposts of the unconscious, are such that he would have difficulty in accepting them. If Joyce had looked at his task in 'Circe' from a strictly Freudian point of view he would have been obliged to include some equivalent of the disguised dream, and so, absurdly, produce material unintelligible to us, let alone to Bloom.

In general, however, if we imagine Bloom being presented with the main theme of these revelations of himself we must also see him in consequence disturbed and incredulous. The waking Bloom, the Bloom of the interior monologues, knows in a rough and ready way that he commonly feels guilty and inferior, and he must be dimly aware of his masochism, but he does not realize the extent to which his life-style is woven out of fear and guilt. How far does Bloom appreciate his proneness to see himself as the object of others' contempt or aggression? On viewing the illustration to *Ruby: the Pride of the Ring* that morning Bloom briefly reflected on cruelty, but apparently was not aware of his disposition to cast himself as victim of Signor Maffei. Similarly, when reading 'Matcham's Masterstroke' Bloom 'envied kindly Mr Beaufoy', who had written the prize-winning story, though we now see that Bloom unconsciously apprehended Philip Beaufoy (the pseudonym of a third-rate writer) as a grand and supercilious fellow looking down on him. Martha and Mary Driscoll, Bloom's collaborator and victim respectively, are top-dogs in the fantasy. He is, or is likely to be, 'on the receiving end'. Unconsciously Bloom is what he, equally unconsciously, thinks others think him to be: if O'Molloy says he's a Mongolian, then he is a Mongol. And while the waking Bloom vaguely feels himself to be an outcast (on account of his Jewishness among other things), he is not aware of his defensive yearnings for high social position. It is possible, too, that the waking Bloom is not keenly aware of his masochism in the technical sense, for nothing similar to the three cruel society beauties elsewhere enters his reveries. Bloom has never asked Molly to whip him or otherwise play the dominant role—or we would learn about it in Molly's soliloquy. We know, as Bloom does not, that Mrs Mervyn Talboys with her hunting crop is an emblem of Bloom's relations with the world.

But Joyce's revolutionary point (implicit in this prodigiously explicit novel) is that Bloom's virtues rest upon this fearful, ignoble, crudely snobbish, sexually squalid foundation. Bloom's gentleness, reasonableness and compassion, his capacity for empathy, his concern for vulnerable people, such as Mrs Purefoy and Stephen, his sporadic courage and political liberalism as displayed in the argument at Barney Kiernan's tavern—these characteristics would not exist without the image of Mrs Mervyn Talboys and her whip. (I am not suggesting that there .is a universal and necessary connection between masochism and certain virtues, but merely that there is a plausible connection of this sort in Joyce's novel.)

At this point we should pause to consider still further why the full Freudian scheme has rarely appealed to novelists. Joyce utilized the scheme, but he utilized so much else besides that his work is not dependent on a particular view of human needs, possibilities and values. Joyce displays the utmost catholicity, and psycho-analysis is merely an element in the mosaic of his work. But a great many other novelists would find it difficult to accept a scheme in which, apparently, the bases of human individuality are not themselves individualized. The traits and quirks of an individual, the singular flavour of that individual, rest it seems on an undifferentiated foundation. What has happened here to the possibility that there is—from birth and perhaps even from the moment of conception—some seed of self-apprehension and self-determination that is already unique? I do not think Freud ever contended against this possibility, and it may be that his work is complementary rather than hostile to it, but certainly the notion of a seed of selfhood entails another kind of unconscious, more appealing to many creative writers.

Selfhood in this sense is unconscious not because we are unaware of it but because it precedes consciousness. Its origins lie in darkness beyond comprehension or analysis. The great proponent of this view was D. H. Lawrence, and indeed it is impossible to grasp some of Lawrence's leading ideas without first grasping this assumption from which the ideas arose. It was an *assumption* in Lawrence, something he felt and never doubted. It is also a widespread assumption, existing in people who do not favour Lawrence's other attitudes. The belief in original selfhood may be mistaken or old-fashioned, a romantic, egotistical development from the Christian concept of the soul; and yet, as we shall see later in this book, it is not incompatible with strands of existentialism. It is worth remarking also that one of the great divides in the modern world is between those who think that we are all alike 'at bottom' and those who think that individuality is fundamental.

Lawrence's *Psychoanalysis and the Unconscious* begins with a denigration of psycho-analysis ('Lawrence *contra* Freud', one might say) and proceeds to an elaborate, eccentric account of the workings of the nervous system. After arguing that Freud's system is an 'ideal' system, a mental attitude towards the sex-instinct and in particular towards incest, Lawrence continues as follows:

What then is the true unconscious? It is not a shadow cast from the mind. It is the spontaneous life-motive in every organism. Where does it begin? It begins where life begins. But that is too vague. It is no use talking about life and the unconscious in bulk. You can talk about electricity, because electricity is a homogeneous force, conceivable apart from any incorporation. But life is inconceivable as a general thing. It exists only in living creatures. So that life begins, now as always, in an individual living creature. In the beginning of the individual living creature is the beginning of life, every time and always, and life has no beginning apart from this. Any attempt at a further generalization takes us merely beyond the consideration of life into the regions of mechanical homogeneous force. This is shown in the cosmologies of eastern religions.

The beginning of life is the beginning of the first individual creature. You may call the naked unicellular bit of plasm the first individual, if you like. Mentally, as far as thinkable simplicity goes, it is the first. So that life begins in the first naked unicellular organism. And where life begins the unconscious also begins. But mark, the first naked unicellular organism is an *individual*. It is a specific individual, not a mathematical unit, like a unit of force.[7]

Three things stand out from this passage: first a misrepresentation of Freud, who did not regard the unconscious solely as a 'shadow cast from the mind' (repression); secondly the absence of any suggestion that human life is a special, superior form of life, and thirdly, the main point that life exists only in individuals. The first item need not detain us. The second brings home to us the fact that Lawrence was the complete antithesis of a humanist. Humanism in all its variants postulates (as does Christianity) that human beings stand apart essentially from animals, but to Lawrence what matters is the individuality of the 'creature'—animal or person. Individuality (or 'soul', for Lawrence sometimes equates the two) is more pronounced in people than in other forms of life, but it exists in lower forms. Then of course there is the more important point that 'life' is not a *general* force, process or quality; it is not something merely manifested in individuals, but something inconceivable apart from individuals.

The unconscious, Lawrence asserts, is 'the spontaneous life-motive in every organism'. Taken on its own the phrase could bring to mind the familiar idea of the life-force, but the rest of the passage rams home the totally different nature of Lawrence's belief. What Lawrence is saying resembles vitalism in respect of the belief that life is something apart from physical and chemical processes, but it differs from vitalism in the insistence on individuality. Life is not an invisible force; it is not an inference from the fact that myriads of things live and grow: it is simply the overt phenomenon of each thing living and growing. And the unconscious is the 'motive' of every living thing. 'Motive' implies intention. Each living thing intends to be itself, and the springs of this intention are naturally unconscious for they either precede consciousness or subsist without it.

In *The Rainbow* Lawrence's heroine, Ursula Brangwen, is troubled by a conversation she has with a woman physicist at Nottingham University College. The physicist contentedly conjectures that life may consist 'in a complexity of physical and chemical activities, of the same order as the activities we already know in science'. A few days later Ursula peers at a 'plant-animal' through a microscope and experiences a sort of vision.

> It [the plant-animal] intended to be itself. But what self? Suddenly in her mind the world gleamed strangely, with an intense light, like the nucleus of the creature under the microscope. Suddenly she had passed away into an intensely-gleaming light of knowledge. She could not understand what it all was. She only knew that it was not limited mechanical energy, nor mere purpose of self-preservation and self-assertion. It was a consummation, a being infinite. Self was a oneness with the infinite. To be oneself was a supreme, gleaming triumph of infinity.[8]

There is something persuasive about this passage, despite one's knowledge as a reader that Ursula has merely seen the animal move. Obviously its movement is not a proof of all that Ursula concludes. In what way can a unicellular creature intend to be itself? One's problem arises from the habit of equating intention with conscious intention, or at best with intention that could be conscious, so the idea of intention in a creature that possesses scarcely one iota of consciousness seems false. At the time Lawrence wrote *The Rainbow* (1915) his belief, as expressed in this passage, was outside the prevailing pattern of psychology, though something rather like the belief can be found today in the writings of many psychologists. At the time of *The Rainbow* the most widely-read psychologists, Freud and Jung, looked backwards in order to explain a person's present behaviour. Their procedure was historical or aetiological. Only Adler, the exponent of individual psychology, explained behaviour in relation to the individual's goals. Thus, according to Adler in his book *The Neurotic Constitution* (1921) a neurosis is an arrangement designed to secure ascendancy over others. The explanation of an attack of anxiety or depression or hysteria lies not in the repressed memories of the patient but in the patient's present desire to secure the attention or submission of friends and family. Clearly, however, Adler's entire will-to-power psychology, with its emphasis on unconscious will and the notion of the inferiority complex, is much more narrowly based than the Lawrentian view that we are now considering. Adler saw people as desiring, consciously or not, to assert themselves over others, whereas Lawrence regarded the very principle of life as a principle of self-determination.

In Lawrence if the unconscious impulse to self-determination is left to itself, then, despite vicissitudes (for life is bound to be a struggle), all is as it should be. To say this is not to suggest that the individual will necessarily be happy, for happiness is beside the point. The important thing is for the individual not to deny the 'God in him', not to allow convention or conscious mental attitudes or plain pusillanimity to impede the impulse to self-determination. Thus Lawrence writes of Walter Morel in *Sons and Lovers* that 'he had denied the God in him' when he has fallen into a state of mindless truculence. Similarly, George Saxton in *The White Peacock* reprehensibly gives up the struggle when, after his rejection by Lettice, the heroine of the novel, he turns to drink and to a resentful form of socialism (since Lettice, a refined bourgeois, has married one of her own class). Morel's own personality withers before his wife's day-by-day onslaught: he cannot become what she wishes him to be, but he cannot sustain his real self either. George Saxton's decline is similarly the result of a blockage of his true path of development.

In Lawrence's novels people are blocked either by a simple failure of the unconscious will or by allowing the conscious will to reign supreme. Lawrence was against the kind of will that says, 'I shall make a million pounds before I'm thirty', or 'I shall become leader of my country', not because such goals are bad, but on the grounds that one's true path of development cannot be mapped out and is certain to be obstructed by rigid adherence to long-term plans. Similarly, Lawrence's respect for the unconscious will led him to reject planned self-control. Thus, when in Chapter XII of *Women in Love* Hermione Roddice boasts of how she overcame her childhood nervousness by will-power, she is told by the hero, Birkin, that 'such a will is an obscenity'. Earlier in the novel (Chapter III) Hermione expounds a doctrine of spontaneity superficially the same as the Lawrentian belief that I am now expounding, but is rudely castigated by Birkin for wanting to have everything in her 'deliberate voluntary consciousness'.

Since one cannot be deliberately spontaneous, it is easy to see the flaw in Hermione; but exactly what did Lawrence advocate? How does the 'true unconscious' work? How are we to recognize the 'spontaneous life-motive' in ourselves or others? The Lawrentian unconscious does not, or does not necessarily, subjugate the intellect: the problem as Lawrence saw it was not the old one of passion versus reason; for Birkin himself is an intellectual, and passion in Lawrence's novels is not always admired. Lawrence was not hostile to conceptual or reflective thinking. For instance, when Hermione Roddice argues that the school-children in *Women in Love* are 'over conscious, burdened to death with concepts', Birkin tells her that the children have too little mind rather than too much. They are 'imprisoned within a limited, false set of concepts'.

The procedure that Lawrence advocated, though it has been

frequently if not usually misunderstood, can be expressed in a straightforward manner. The human mind by its very nature invents, receives, or entertains concepts. This faculty cannot be done away with: we cannot live like animals from the instincts or impulses alone. Nevertheless, the mind can be in error, whereas the dynamic unconscious will cannot be assessed in terms of good and evil, correctness and incorrectness. The mind can be in error simply through overlooking or distorting the facts of the situation, but it can also lead us astray by setting up some concept that inhibits the unconscious will. Indeed all concepts to a greater or lesser extent inhibit the unconscious will, so the task must always be to modify the concept. The unconscious will is what in some contexts Lawrence calls 'the blood'. By 'the blood' he does not simply mean passion, carnality or libido; he does not mean instinct in the proper sense of aggression, hunger, self-preservation, sex, and so on. He means just this self-determining impulse that we are talking about.

Lawrence's belief can best be understood by first referring to some remarks in the Foreword to *Fantasia of the Unconscious*.

And finally, it seems to me that even art is utterly dependent on philosophy: or if you prefer it, on a metaphysic. The metaphysic or philosophy may not be anywhere very accurately stated and may be quite unconscious, in the artist, yet it is a metaphysic that governs men at the time, and is by all men more or less comprehended, and lived. Men live and see according to some gradually developing and gradually withering vision. This vision exists also as a dynamic idea or metaphysics—exists first as such. Then it is unfolded into life and art.[9]

There are some difficulties in this passage, and some apparent contradictions of remarks made elsewhere by Lawrence, but the broad idea is not affected by these. Lawrence is referring primarily to art but he makes it clear that the thesis is not confined to art. He is saying simply that we are guided by ideas, whether we know it or not, but when an idea ceases to be satisfactory it must be altered or abandoned. It is like starting out with a map and changing the details on the map every time the map fails to match the terrain. We need a map to get going at all, but it is absurd to stick to it when it is contradicted by our experiences on the journey.

'Men live and see according to some gradually developing and gradually withering vision.' The vision referred to is partly collective and partly individual. More precisely, the individual vision will usually be a private, somewhat peculiar version of the collective vision. Sometimes the private vision will be (as with Blake in the

38

late eighteenth century) wildly different from the collective. At all events, it is the private vision that counts, that must serve as a map for the individual. But this vision or map, whether it tends to uphold or to challenge the collective, must be subject to continual modifications. Thus visions gradually develop and gradually wither.

The vision of an individual, insofar as it is peculiar to him, is an approximate expression of his unconscious will, his 'true unconscious'. The unconscious will throws up into the mind a concept or certain patterns of imagery and feeling (a 'metaphysic', as Lawrence calls it), and this 'upper' manifestation of the unconscious will enables the individual to feel his way forward. It constitutes perhaps his sense of identity. But he should be prepared to let his unconscious will throw up amendments from time to time, and move his conscious notions ever away from approximation to accuracy. There are three distinct traps one can fall into. The first is the obvious one of failing to notice any discrepancy between the private vision and the collective. We cannot all use the same map, for while we are all going in the same direction, each person should be following his own route. The second trap is the subtler one of sustaining the old vision even when (as is almost continually happening) the 'true unconscious' proposes modifications. Here the individual is like one who sticks to the old map however often it causes him to stumble or lose his way. (It is reasonable to guess that such stumbling or losing one's bearings as a result of inordinate reliance on a fixed notion would be Lawrence's explanation of neurosis.)

So far perhaps we have merely cleared the ground. We have, for instance, disposed of the belief that Lawrence was blankly hostile to ideas, to intellect. We are still left without a clear view of what Lawrence meant by the 'spontaneous life-motive'; that is, his version of the unconscious. The difficulty lies in the fact that, by definition, the spontaneous life-motive is not a general phenomenon, so it can hardly be described in general terms. The best procedure is to draw examples from Lawrence's novels and stories of persons succeeding or failing by the author's test.

Ursula Brangwen in *The Rainbow* assuredly lives from her 'true unconscious'. Hers is a chequered career from childhood to early maturity, and she makes numerous mistakes—falling in love with the wrong people, taking up the wrong profession—but she is animated continually by inner impulses towards personal growth. These impulses can be partially explained in the common quasi-Freudian manner, by reference to parental influences for example, but they cannot be entirely so explained. Thus it is clear that Ursula would never have become the questing individual she is but for a certain lack of fulfilment in her father and a consequent unease in her parents' marriage. But the precise nature of Ursula's questing is inexplicable: it arises before and directs her conscious deliberations, and therefore constitutes the operations of the true unconscious.

As a child Ursula rejects the collective vision that church and Sunday-school would impose upon her, and forms her own image of Christ, an image of pride, fierceness and splendour. There is no reflection or attitudinising involved here, in the manner of a conventionally unconventional adolescent: the image of the proud, fierce Jesus arises naturally, years before the awakening of the sceptical intellect. Ursula simply recognizes in her childish way that a gentle Jesus is inimical to her self-development.

At school she loves learning—algebra, French verbs, poetry are all grist to her mill. Again, this love of learning owes nothing to the home environment and little enough, except for the bare opportunity, to school itself. But when in due course Ursula arrives at University College, Nottingham, though her desires are satisfied for the first year, they are thwarted in the second. She comes to feel that the college is a sham, a place in which 'the religious virtue of knowledge was become a flunkey to the god of material success'. Consequently Latin, Old English and French, once so exciting to her, grow stale. This is not just boredom or culpable restlessness, but a recognition that her way forward, though it will continue to include learning, cannot be along this academic path. A similar pattern of enthusiasm followed by rejection is displayed in her love-affairs with Skrebensky, the conventional army officer, and Winifred Inger, the lesbian schoolmistress.

What happens in all Ursula's lungings and withdrawals is that she turns aside from whatever does not aid her growth. She is like a plant moving upwards through the earth and circumventing stones or other materials that stand in its way. And, of course, like a plant Ursula cannot say where she is going, but unlike a plant she has to form provisional notions. The procedure is creative: the artist works away at his canvas, trying to solve this technical problem and that, but does not know what the solution will be until he finds it, at which time the nature of the main problem itself is retrospectively illuminated.

Lawrence was advocating a creative mode of life, even for those (like Ursula) who have no creative talent in any recognized sense. The principle seems to be one of spotting whatever genuinely excites you and shifting away from whatever seems dead. If the excitement is genuine, it will owe nothing to fabricated attitudes or doctrines. At the same time, the principle is not selfishly individualistic, as may be concluded from the brief account I have given, and as has often been supposed. There is individualism of a sort in Lawrence's views, certainly, but this individualism is integrally connected with concern for the social world. Most of the heroes and heroines of Lawrence's novels after *Sons and Lovers* are intensely occupied with the state of society. *The Rainbow, Women in Love, Aaron's Rod, Kangaroo,* and *The Plumed Serpent* are all plainly about social matters, and so are many of the short stories, poems and essays. In *Lady Chatterley's Lover* Connie and Mellors do not escape to the woods from the world of the pits and the shabby Midlands towns, in a manner reminiscent of the popular romances of the period, but, rather, their sexual activities (necessarily conducted in out-of-the-way places) are seen as a means of repairing the ravages to the human psyche produced by industrialization.

Lawrence's 'individualism' consisted of a belief that the problems of society can be cured only by private individuals in their private relations with one another. To put the matter more comprehensively, if a sufficient number of people learn to live from the 'true unconscious' in each one of them, then the social world will come to reflect their needs. The drive is against the categories and abstractions with which the language of 'social concern' is usually larded. Mechanization is the modern enemy, and so thoroughly have mechanical concepts become woven into the texture of our thinking, that the palliatives we propose are themselves liable to be mechanical.

In comparatively recent years a body of thinking has grown up which recalls in some respects these earlier ideas of Lawrence. Some psychologists and social theorists, especially in America, have been saying similar things about the need for private regeneration and the importance of creativity. A survey of this latter-day movement must be left to a later chapter, but it is desirable that the ideas of one American psychologist, Abraham Maslow, be included here. Maslow's major work, *Motivation and Personality,* came out in 1954, and it contains (along with much else that must be mentioned later on) a chapter entitled 'Higher and Lower Needs', which postulates that the need to grow or develop creatively, somewhat in the manner that Lawrence advocated, is instinctive, that is, it is unconscious in origins, of central importance and finally irremovable. In effect, Maslow, a neo-Freudian, said that Freud's version of the unconscious was not so much wrong as incomplete, since the instinctual drives of which the unconscious is made up include a drive towards self-enhancement. This, in addition to being a means for us of linking the seemingly opposed views of Lawrence and Freud, is a distinctly novel attitude. For the old thinking took it for granted (as we have noted in the preceding chapter) that man's instincts were different from, and often destructive of, his higher aspirations. Freud's own innovation was to argue that such aspirations are sublimations of instincts, but now Maslow argues that the impulse to self-development is as instinctual as the impulse to gratify basic needs for sex, food and so on.

Maslow writes:

The recognition that man's best impulses are appreciably intrinsic, rather than fortuitous and relative, must have tremendous implication for value theory. It means, for one thing, that it is no longer either necessary or desirable to deduce values by logic or to try to read them off from authorities or revelations. All we need do, apparently, is to observe and research. Human nature carries within itself the answer to the questions, how can I be good: how can I be happy: how can I be fruitful? The organism tells us what it needs (and therefore what it values) by sickening when deprived of these values and by growing when not deprived.[10]

The biological emphasis of the last sentence of this passage very well matches Lawrence's belief in a 'true unconscious' as opposed to an unconscious that is a 'shadow cast from the mind'. Man as total organism, rather than as mind-in-a-body, requires not only sustenance and sex but also an avenue of fruitfulness. Lawrence's novels are largely about human organisms growing or sickening in consequence of an interaction between the unconscious bases of the organism and the environment—which includes, of course, those conscious ideas that are in part products of the environment.

There is more to be said about developing notions of the unconscious in the twentieth century, for so far we have barely glanced at the ideas of Jung. Again it is Lawrence who, among creative writers, best illustrates some sort of correspondence between artistic, intuitive beliefs and the findings of psychology.

3

THE LIVING SELF

Integration of the Personality in Lawrence and Jung

There is no evidence that Jung was acquainted with the writings of Lawrence, and Lawrence's infrequent references to Jung do not suggest that he was much impressed by the psychologist. In fact the most revealing reference is rather contemptuous.

> Jung is very interesting, in his own sort of fat muddled mystical way. Although he may be an initiate and a thrice-sealed adept, he's soft somewhere, and I've no doubt you'd find it fairly easy to bring his heavy posterior down with a bump off his apple-cart. I think Gourdjieff would be a tougher nut.[1]

So Lawrence saw Jung's works as comparable with theosophy (which Jung actually despised), and of course many other people have been similarly sceptical of much of Jung's teaching—or, alternatively, have professed themselves mystified by it. Both men have had ardent disciples and detractors. For some critics Lawrence is the outstandingly perceptive explorer of the modern moral consciousness; for others his writings are riddled with eccentricities and perversities. Similarly, Jung's work has brought into being the many institutes and societies of analytical psychology (as well as providing non-Jungian psychologists with valuable attitudes and insights), while being met with disbelief or even derision in other schools of thought. Jung's work as a whole forms a vast quasi-religious system, stern though optimistic, and designed to meet the spiritual demands of the modern world. On the other hand, Lawrence was an abominator of systems, yet his work has a general consistency, enveloping minor inconsistencies, which amounts to a sort of doctrine. It is not surprising that Lawrence, despite his sneers, found Jung 'very interesting', because he must have discerned amid the 'fat muddled mystical' elements strands of thinking relevant to his own search. Each man, differently equipped and by a different route, ventured into the same territory in pursuit of a similar prize.

If any single figure can be said to stand behind them both, it is probably Nietszche. Behind Lawrence he is shadowy, inexplicit, a philosophic precursor whose ideas are certainly not simply accepted but form an appropriate well-spring of 'post-Christian' thought. Jung repeatedly acknowledges his youthful interest in Nietszche, but just as often tells us where the philospher went wrong, why he went mad in the end. What Nietszche principally did that was of interest to both Lawrence and Jung was to tilt against the old Christian symbols, looking for a way that would admit the claims of Dionysus, a figure who summed up for Nietszche much of what Jung means by the unconscious (especially the Collective Unconscious) and what Lawrence means by the Flesh. Nietszche saw Christianity as a long, disastrous episode in the history of the human race. Jung, on the other hand, regarded Christianity as an inevitable and profitable phase, whose traditional symbols were for many people losing their vitality. He believed that for modern man, at least, the Trinity should be a Quaternity, including the Devil. Lawrence continually asserted that Christ was—to use the language of *The Plumed Serpent*—lord of the one way, up to heaven, whereas we needed a lord of the two ways, up to heaven and down to the earthy depths of man's nature.

Both Lawrence and Jung sought a new method of integrating the personality, since they regarded the old methods—through the Church, settled communities, a sense of tradition, feelings of kinship with nature—as breaking down. To each of them the enthronement of consciousness and ratiocination was chief among the fallacies that they wished to correct. To Lawrence this fallacy was so much part and parcel of industrialization and the rise of science, in other words the irreversible trend of modern life, that fury and desperation sometimes inform his writing. He felt himself embattled and sometimes he felt himself losing. Jung, however, was perfectly happy with science and much less disturbed generally by the twentieth century. Another difference lies in their methods of dealing with personal problems. For Lawrence such problems were worked out, as one would expect, in his writings, and they continued to the end of his days to act as obstacles as well as inspirations. Jung experienced some emotional difficulties in childhood and adolescence, and later, at the time of the First World War, went through a near-psychotic phase. But he acquired a sort of easy intercourse with manifestations of his unconscious, and seems to have had a fairly serene existence after the age of about forty. To each of them, it should be added, a new way of integrating the personality was a religious enterprise: the result, never to be wholly realized, would be a re-discovery of God.

Jung's notion of the process of 'individuation' has many times been expounded by adherents so that a general grasp of it is readily obtainable. The process takes place in two phases. First there is the youthful phase in which a man is normally occupied in strengthening his ego and his 'persona' (roughly speaking, his outer social personality) and by so doing coming to realistic terms with everyday life. The second phase, which is likely to begin (if it begins at all) in middle age, is a much more profound activity. What it consists of, very broadly, is a shifting of understanding of oneself downwards, so to speak, so that unconscious elements are acknowledged, even if they cannot be, in the narrower senses of the word, understood. It is important to realize (in connection with Lawrence as well as with Jung) that the unconscious is primary: it comes first in the process of evolution, in recorded history and in the growth of an individual from childhood. It remains the source of psychic energy and the 'place' (spatial metaphors are convenient, though they have probably been misleading) where vital meaning resides. Our characteristic modern error lies in the assumption that meaning is 'in', or can be apprehended by, the normal processes of the conscious mind.

To Jung (as to Freud) a person is not wholly, or even largely, what he consciously thinks he is: on the contrary the unconscious, which is more commodious and more in tune with the true nature of things than the conscious mind, contains compensatory elements that are also part of the real man. For instance, a man who, in Jungian terms, belongs to the introvert type and whose most developed function happens to be thinking, is relatively unaware of his feelings. He is poor at distinguishing or defining his feelings: they are comparatively 'undifferentiated'. But his feelings are as much a part of him as his conscious, rational highly differentiated thoughts. In general, if the conscious processes of an individual are mistaken, moving in the wrong direction, then the unconscious provides compensatory messages, in the form of dreams for example.

It should be added at this point that Jung distinguished four mental functions: thinking, feeling, intuition and sensation. Thinking and feeling form a pair, one element of which predominates in any individual. Intuition and sensation form an auxiliary pair, and again each person develops one of them more than the other. Ideally, as a man grows beyond youth he should discover, first, which is his predominant function of the first pair, and later try to understand the natures and claims of his other functions, so that they no longer operate blindly within him.

But more important for our purposes is the concept, not unique to Jung but strongly emphasized by him, of the Collective Unconscious, the components of which can never be known, in the ordinary sense. These components, termed 'archetypes', are common to the entire human race, though in their 'upper' manifestations (that is insofar as they or their effects reach the sphere of the 'Personal Unconscious') they take on the peculiarities of the individual. The most accessible archetype, the archetype most readily apprehended by a man who is prepared for the second and more profound stage of individuation, Jung called the 'Shadow'. As a collective phenomenon the Shadow has in the past been personified as the Devil or other representatives of evil, of 'darkness', of the tendencies rejected by a race or a culture. In the sphere of the Personal Unconscious a man's Shadow takes on his own attributes, but of course they are the attributes that he has disowned. The individual's Shadow, in other words, consists at one level of precisely those impulses and attitudes that he personally regards as bad and that he tends to discover in other, less admirable persons.

The second archetype is the 'Anima' (or 'Animus', for a woman), and this consists of the contra-sexual tendencies in an individual. Every man, says Jung, has his feminine side, hidden from himself and others. At bottom the Anima is an image, or a cluster of images, of womankind; but at the personal level each man's Anima will consist of his own notions of feminineness. And these notions are likely to be imbued with his Shadow-qualities, the qualities which he regards as inferior or wicked. 'Therefore,' writes a leading Jungian exponent, 'in principle an abstract scientist's anima will be primitive, emotional, and romantic, while that of the intuitive, sensitive artist will be a down-to-earth, sensual type.'[2]

The task for a man engaged in the process of individuation is first to become as aware as possible of the existence and nature of his Shadow and subsequently to become similarly aware of his Anima. In this way he grows in understanding of his psychical make-up, an advance that not only benefits him immensely but also contributes to the social good, since it becomes less and less possible for him to assume that evil is 'out there', in other persons, classes or races.

Lying behind the Shadow and the Anima (with its Shadow-attributes) are the fundamental archetypes of Wise Old Man and Magna Mater. The first of these, representing the spiritual principle, lies in the innermost recesses of a man; the second, representing the material principle, may be discovered deep within a woman. Thus Jung in traditional manner links spirit with maleness and matter with femaleness. There are plain mythological versions of these concepts, for instance the magician or prophet on the one hand, and the fertility goddess or sibyl on the other.

When a man has progressed so far that he has acknowledged and apprehended the foregoing archetypes in his own make-up, he is ready for the last stage of his spiritual journey. Having come to terms with his 'dark' side and his feminine qualities, and having discovered his relationship with spirit and with matter (that is, primordial nature), he is theoretically capable of proceeding to a final unification of the conscious and unconscious areas of his psyche, through occupying a mid-way point between them, called by Jung the 'Self'. One who has reached this point has been transformed, re-born. The Self may be thought of as one's tiny share of God-hood; it is probably to be compared with the Hindu concept of the Atman, the indwelling spirit that partakes of the nature of the universal spirit or Brahman. Reaching the Self does not bring the end of trouble and sorrow, but it does bring a considerable lessening of egotistical sufferings and a total absence of neurosis. It brings also a sense of identification with the world at large, so that, by a seeming paradox, the more a man becomes himself, the more he realizes his identity with the rest of nature.

This brief summary of material that is presented elaborately from varying points of view in several of Jung's works (and most comprehensively in *Symbols of Transformation*, *The Archetypes and the Collective Unconscious*, and *The Integration of the Personality*) is sufficient for us to begin an examination of some relevant features of Lawrence's writings. What follows is not a Jungian analysis of Lawrence, for such a project would be over-long and over-ambitious, but simply a consideration of Lawrence in the light of Jung's ideas. I shall be concerned with Lawrence's intentions and how far these turn out to match Jung's beliefs. The kinship is partly due to the period of social and philosophical history in which both men worked; that is, a period fundamentally characterized by the shocking discovery (or re-discovery, without God as bastion or Devil as scapegoat) of the 'dark' side of man's nature.

Lawrence's childhood—and indeed his whole life—was deeply affected not solely by the intense relationship with his mother, but also by what he came to regard as a reversal of roles by his parents. Those who regard the notion of masculine and feminine roles as mere cultural conditioning might see no inevitable problem here, but Lawrence held more traditional views. He believed in fact in a biological norm of male leadership, a good illustration of which in the novels is provided by Birkin in *Women in Love*. Birkin becomes something of an avatar to Ursula Brangwen, though he brings spiritual illumination to her (and to himself) by carnal means. But of course Birkin is a swimmer against the tide of social forces, not least in his refusal to yield to the female principle. He is quite exceptional, the generality of men being either no leaders or false leaders. Morel in *Sons and Lovers* is much more typical, for Lawrence believed, or came to believe, that conditions in his own childhood

47

home were, for all their specific features, symptomatic of a wide-spread condition. In the modern period men had ceased to fulfil the venturesome male function, so that their women-folk, frenziedly and without deep conviction, had taken up the reins.

> Once man vacates his camp of sincere, passionate positivity in disinterested being, his supreme responsibility to fulfil his own profoundest impulses, with reference to none but God or his own soul, not taking woman into count at all, in this primary responsibility to his own deepest soul; once man vacates this strong citadel of his own genuine, not spurious, divinity, then in comes woman, picks up the sceptre and begins to conduct a rag-time band.[3]

This is how the older Lawrence saw the basis of the parental situation he had portrayed years earlier in *Sons and Lovers*. His mother's assumption of ethical guardianship, his father's neglect of all such responsibilities, were indicative of a general malaise. Of Walter Morel in the novel Lawrence writes that he had 'denied the God in him', but there is at this stage little suggestion that Morel's denial is but one form of an extensive male helplessness. Nevertheless we sense that Mrs Morel's heroism is distorted, not simply because it is sometimes cruel or blind, but for some more fundamental reason which is nowhere explained. The young Lawrence writing the book either did not fully realize or did not wish to emphasize that the mother falls back on respectability, diatribes against the demon drink and so on, in the absence, not just of ordinarily decent behaviour from her husband, but also of the subtler moral pioneering that she is bound to expect of him. Morel is not to be blamed, for he is baffled; but so are most men.

The original foreword to *Sons and Lovers* generalizes the problems in the Morel family, though the story itself does not. In that foreword (a letter of 1913 to Edward Garnett) Lawrence maintains that in the beginning was the Flesh, not the Word. Writing in Biblical manner, he asserts that God the Father, the ground of all being, must be Flesh: the Word, which was Jesus, was secondary, a later emanation. Furthermore, God the Father ought strictly speaking to be God the Mother. He (or She, for Lawrence himself deliberately mixes up the pronouns) is the primordial and infinite ground, ever-changing but changeless; but the Word is strictly finite, appropriate only to times, places and even to individuals. Now the man, if he is to be truly a man, should go out into the world at large and utter the Word, his Word, but never lose connection with the primordial ground which should be manifested in his mother or his wife. Lawrence uses the metaphor of a bee-hive.

And the bee, who is a Son, comes home to his Queen as to the Father, in service and humility, for suggestion, and renewal, and identification which is the height of his glory, for begetting. And again the bee goes forth to attend the flowers, the Word in his pride and masterfulness of new strength and new wisdom. And as he comes and goes, so shall man for ever come and go; to his work, his uttering, wherein he is masterful and proud; come home to his woman, through whom is God the Father, and who is herself, whether she will have it or not, God the Father, before whom the man in his hour is full of reverence, and in whom he is glorified and hath the root of his pride.[4]

From these words, written at the time of the publication of *Sons and Lovers*, we can see that the novel implies a Jungian problem in addition to—or correlative with—the more obvious Freudian (Oedipal) problem. It is not simply that Paul loves his mother and hates his father, but that his mother is obliged to combine two roles, to act as worker bee and as Queen Bee. But as a woman her utterances of the Word are—in the Lawrentian view—inevitably trite, inadequate. The same may be said of Miriam Leivers and even, to some extent, of Clara Dawes. For one of the noteworthy things about the novel is its presentation of women who usurp what Lawrence later saw as the male function. The situation between Miriam and her brothers resembles the situation between Mrs Morel and her husband, at least in that the woman in each case strives for conscious knowledge while her menfolk stand by, indifferent and jeering. One of Miriam's ambiguous features is that she wishes to guide Paul's genius by her own shallower insights. She knows, though she cannot possibly know, what form Paul's genius should take, and even what sort of an individual he should become. Miriam, in short, is another who has abandoned her queenly role and gone forth, inadequately equipped, as a worker bee. Clara Dawes, on the other hand, has retained enough awareness of her true function to satisfy a vital need in Paul, but she too has a spiritually inadequate husband (Baxter Dawes is not unlike Morel) and is keen on women's rights. The point is not that Lawrence was hostile to the suffragette movement but that he regarded it as an attempt by women to break out of a cultural impasse reached under male leadership. However, this proposed way out was as mentalistic, as 'masculine', as the way in.

In the early writings of Lawrence we are faced with his stumbling first steps along the path of 'individuation'; steps taken intuitively without benefit of Jung's theories, but which the theories (formulated for the most part years later) help to explain. In Jungian terminology, the Shadow side of a nature so intuitive, so quiveringly sensitive as

Lawrence's would be coarse, unseeing, perhaps brutal. An Anima-figure for Lawrence, corresponding to the fundamental Anima-image within him, would have a certain brashness, unabashed sensuality; she would tend to be nerveless, accepting, possibly hedonistic. What Lawrence did not know at the time of writing *Sons and Lovers* was that men like his father and Baxter Dawes were partly composed of qualities that he needed to come to terms with in himself. At the same time he was insufficiently aware that the impressive women of his early life, his mother and Jessie Chambers, were not true Anima-figures for him. But there are suggestions in the book that he is feeling his way through to recognition of these facts. If I am not mistaken, Morel, the father, is treated with more sympathetic understanding than Lawrence realized, and certainly a curious kinship grows up between Paul and his obvious opposite, Baxter Dawes. Critics have sometimes detected a homosexual element in the friendship between Paul and Dawes, relating this element to the more plainly homosexual feelings between Cyril and George Saxton in *The White Peacock*. Such considerations may provide a different dimension but do not, I think, alter one's understanding of the basic situation. Lawrence, in regularly producing figures of comparatively mindless male potency, from George Saxton and Annable through to Mellors (whether ruined like Saxton or chirpily surviving like Mellors), was trying to accommodate his own Shadow-attributes.

No one has been able to explain Lawrence's gamekeepers, Annable and Mellors, in ordinary biographical terms, as possibly based upon an actual person or incident. Yet Annable, at least, requires some sort of explanation. He is almost superfluous in *The White Peacock*, though the title is taken from his remarks, and Cyril's conversation with him in the ruined chapel is both potent and enigmatic, like a dream. It is very probable that Annable was a pure fantasy-product from Lawrence's unconscious, a figure that the author did not understand, but recognized as important to the book and to himself. Mellors, as a late and much more consciously contrived character derived from Annable, can perhaps be seen as a measure of the advance in self-knowledge that Lawrence had made in the intervening years.

The other side of Lawrence's early task was to replace the false Anima-figures with true ones. He began *Sons and Lovers* (then called 'Paul Morel') in October, 1910; the next month he broke off his 'betrothal' to Jessie Chambers; in the December he became engaged to the Ilkeston girl, Louie Burrows, and Mrs Lawrence died. The move from Jessie Chambers to Louie Burrows (upon whom Ursula Brangwen was partly based) was a move in the right direction, but it was not until 1912 that Lawrence met his perfect Anima-figure in the person of Frieda Weekley. It is well known that Frieda assisted him with the completion of *Sons and Lovers*, and generally assumed that she came on the scene too late to help him clarify the personal problems at the core of the book. But what she undoubtedly did was to foster his development in the right way. In a letter of this period Lawrence wrote: 'I shan't let F. leave me, if I can help it. I feel I've got a mate and I'll fight tooth and claw to keep her. She says I'm reverting, but I'm not—I'm only coming out wholesome and myself.'[5] Frieda was able to do this, to produce such an exultant sense of self-actualization in Lawrence, because she was precisely the brazen aristocrat whom his soul, hitherto fed on provincial pieties, required.[6]

In this phase of his life Lawrence was undergoing the process of detachment from his mother, a process that Jung maintains is more difficult for modern Westernized man than it is among some primitive peoples, who practise initiation rites and ceremonies for precisely that purpose. For Lawrence the process was especially difficult, and some critics believe that he never completed it. But whether he did or not, it is clear that Lawrence, in his life and in his books, did plumb beneath the image of womankind provided by his mother to a deeper aspect of his own contra-sexual tendencies. For Frieda, like the heroines of some of his novels and stories after *Sons and Lovers*, possessed the Shadow-qualities which matched Lawrence's own. According to Aldous Huxley, who knew the Lawrences particularly well, Frieda was 'profoundly matter of fact, accepting events as they were given, in all their painful or delightful confusion'.[7] She was impatient with ideals and had almost no notion of inhibiting her basic impulses in accordance with doctrines or principles. Lawrence's 'best' women in the novels—Ursula Brangwen, Kate Leslie, Constance Chatterley—have more in common with Frieda than with Mrs Lydia Lawrence; whereas the reverse is true of his 'worst' women, such as Hermione Roddice or Doña Carlota.

But in the period immediately following the publication of *Sons and Lovers* Lawrence was still engaged with the problem of women's failure to find suitable male leadership. He was coming to know the qualities and needs of his own feminine side, and he began to apply these to the actual sphere of women in society. Accordingly, the second half of his next novel, *The Rainbow*, presents a heroine rather than a hero facing the challenges of the contemporary world. Ursula Brangwen, whose nature contains Anima elements, likes as a child to regard herself as one of the Biblical 'daughters of men' who will one day be taken by one of the 'Sons of God', but in the novel this grand consummation (as opposed to ordinary sexual consummation) does not occur: her lover, Skrebensky, is conventional, a failure to her. Lawrence evidently could not at this stage provide a suitable mate for Ursula, because such a man, by definition, would have been one who held the solution to her problems. What this amounts to is that Lawrence had first to work out what the feminine side of his own nature required, and then, upon the basis of such requirements, re-form the 'upper', masculine side of his nature. His earlier self-representations were now hopelessly unequal to the task. ('I hate Paul Morel', wrote Lawrence in a letter of this period; and one imagines that he must have hated Cyril Beardsall of *The White Peacock* even more.)

The Rainbow does not, of course, present a straightforward pattern illustrating some simple thesis about questing women as against spiritually dormant men. In the first generation of Brangwens with which the novel deals, Tom Brangwen, the barely literate farmer, is obscurely dissatisfied with the Ilkeston girls whom he might marry and turns instead to the Polish widow, Lydia Lensky, who worships 'God as a Mystery' and is a faintly Magna-Mater figure. It is Tom who asks the questions, so to speak, and Lydia who, partially at least, soothes his restless spirit. In the second generation Anna Lensky, daughter of Lydia and step-daughter of Tom, conducts her own exploration only to the stage of bearing her second child. At that time she comes to regard herself as a 'threshold' over which others, her children, will pass to further adventures. She herself has resigned from the adventure, while her husband, Will, has proved to be regressive, concerned only with the obsolescent Christian symbols. In this way it is left to Ursula, the eldest child of Will and Anna, to confront the turmoil of Lawrence's own period.

There is one striking difference pertinent to our theme between the second half of *The Rainbow* and its successor, *Women in Love*, and that is the changed function of Ursula. Almost everything in the last nine chapters of *The Rainbow* is seen from Ursula's point of view, whereas in *Women in Love* she is merely one of four principal characters, acting out their intertwined, complex, and sometimes ambivalent destinies. In particular, Ursula is in some senses subordinate to Birkin. During the course of the novel she, as one of the daughters of men, finds her son of God in Birkin, whose confused argumentation and preaching constitute Lawrence's painful re-formation of his upper, masculine side. Whenever Birkin and Ursula are on the scene together, we sense that Lawrence is with Birkin, viewing Ursula as a person apart (though naturally the empathy with Ursula is very thoroughgoing). All Ursula's doubts, questions and downright hostility in the face of Birkin's assertions about the two of them and about society in general are not simply reproductions of Frieda's attitudes (real or imagined), but precisely the inner doubts which Lawrence needed to allay. Ursula is not Frieda or any actual woman, except perhaps in a few incidental ways, but at least a partial representation of Lawrence's Anima, his indwelling image of womankind; and the conversations between Birkin and her are in effect dialogues between self and soul.

I use the word, 'self', here only in its common meaning of ego or ego-consciousness, while using the word, 'soul', more or less in the Jungian sense in which 'soul-image' is a synonym for Anima. Jung's specialized notion of the 'Self', on the other hand, as a mid-way point between consciousness and the unconscious is exactly what Lawrence, in the portraits of Birkin and Ursula, was striving to reach. At this point in Lawrence's career the similarity between the doctrine towards which he was groping and the doctrine later expounded by Jung begins to emerge. Partly through Birkin's words and partly by the dramatic enactments of the novel, we learn that society is in a state of dissolution, because men and women are out of touch with nature, which is God. There is the possibility of an apocalypse, out of which new life will emerge, but Birkin comes to believe that he and Ursula should fight against the general drift. The mode of combat is to pursue one's deepest desires, thus moving along the road to Being. The ideal of *imitatio Christi* is dead (as Jung also argues in *Modern Man in Search of a Soul*), and people are without a guide. In this uncertainty they opt either for meaningless conventionality or for some form of self-destruction. The destructive people in the novel, notably Gudrun, Gerald, Hermione and Loerke (though almost everyone is implicated in the general rot), are outstanding individuals, but each in a different way aspires not to Being, but to thinghood. Gerald and Gudrun exploit each other, and this leads to Gerald's death and to a state of mind bordering on madness in Gudrun. Hermione has cultivated an 'obscene' form of will-power that subjugates her real, largely unconscious will, so that there is a 'void, an insufficiency of being within her'. Loerke is the extreme destructive figure in that he contrives, as far as possible, to reduce his own and other people's complex personalities to the level of a mere stream of sensations. He is one form (a perverted form) of the Lawrentian Shadow-figure. His name, as F. R. Leavis has suggested,[8] may be derived from Loki, the demon of the Sagas, whom Jung specifically mentions as an expression of the Shadow in literature.

Birkin maintains that the drift of the time (the immediate pre-war years) is towards 'destructive creation', in other words the discovery of new methods of analysis, of splitting or disintegration. There are two broad channels of destructive creation, one being the north-European way of 'ice-destructive knowledge', and the other being the 'African' way of 'ultimate *physical* consciousness, mindless, utterly sensual'. The first of these means overvaluation of the conscious mind, while the second means the attempted annihilation of the conscious mind. Birkin's countervailing struggle towards 'synthetic creation' and his advocacy of 'single being' are, speaking generally, quite in accordance with Jung's belief in 'differentiating' as far as possible the four functions of thinking, feeling, intuition and sensation, and in achieving a balance between the conscious and unconscious minds. But Birkin's precise way of arriving at 'accession into being' for him and Ursula—namely buggery—is a piece of Lawrentian oddity, amenable to those Freudian rather than Jungian methods of analysis that Jung himself maintained are more appropriate to certain stages of an individual's development.

However, there is no pretence in *Women in Love* that an ultimate answer has been found to the problems that the book exposes. At the close Birkin tells a sceptical Ursula that he wanted 'eternal union' with a man as well as with her. Naturally this too has been seen as an expression of latent homosexuality in Lawrence, but such a view is superficial even if it is correct. What Lawrence was really after is made plainer by the succeeding novels from *Aaron's Rod* to *The Plumed Serpent*. Three of these four novels emphatically include relationships between men, but do so in contexts that show that Lawrence's basic drive was not towards anything resembling ordinary homosexual unions, but towards further insight into his own psyche as a means of self-unification. From this would inevitably follow a prescription for mankind, since in such a writer as Lawrence, philosophical even when he is most local and specific, concerned for society even when he is most self-centred, the cure of his own soul and the cure of the world's soul are identical.

Put briefly, Lawrence sought greater understanding of the relationship between his own 'dark' aspects of Shadow and Anima on the one hand, and his 'light', masculine ego on the other. Each of the next four novels constitutes a different kind of foray into this terrain, and the deepest penetration is achieved by *The Plumed Serpent*.

In *Aaron's Rod* Lawrence brings a sensitive, artistic ex-miner, Aaron Sissons, into contact with a remarkable man, Lilly, who appears to be wise and penetrating. Aaron, a gentle, rather feminine individual (though not in the least effeminate), is an idealized version of Lawrence's 'soul-image'; while Lilly is an idealized representation of Lawrence in his 'upper' capacity as utterer of the Word. Neither of these characters has much to do with any actual persons whom Lawrence knew, though the basis of Aaron's story was suggested by an actual occurrence and several of the minor characters were taken from life. In writing the novel Lawrence's fundamental procedure was to personify two complementary aspects of his own nature, and to cause one of the personifications—Aaron —to encounter various unsatisfactory manifestations of the postwar world. But Lilly, whom Aaron meets about half way through the book, is also unsatisfactory. The implication of the conversations between Aaron and Lilly is that Lilly is right, but only so far as his thinking goes. Something is missing. Aaron refuses to submit to Lilly, even though at one point he has seen Lilly as his 'mind's hero'. Despite this, Aaron is left at the end with ideas remarkably like the doctrine according to Lilly. It is not an adequate doctrine, but merely the best the author can manage for the moment. In effect, here is one more dialogue between Lawrence's self and soul in which the former fails to satisfy the latter.

The Lost Girl, Lawrence's next published novel (though it was begun as early as 1913) is an attempt at a different solution. The author's ego-consciousness is no longer inside the story, in the guise of a character like Birkin or like Lilly, but remains outside interpreting the events, and one result of this is the social comedy of the opening chapters. Alvina Houghton, the protagonist, is rather more a straightforwardly naturalistic character than a projection of part of Lawrence's psyche, though she has Anima attributes. Cicio Marasco is quite another matter: he is Lawrence's attempt to depict what Alvina calls a 'Dark master from the Underworld', in other words Shadow qualities of pure instinct, of brutishness. Throughout his career, but with varying degrees of urgency, Lawrence evidently felt the need to accommodate these qualities in his writings, even as so many other writers have done. The Shadow, when he appears in literature, has usually been an obviously bad or inferior person (such as Mephistopheles, Caliban, Frankenstein's monster or Mr Hyde) towards whom, nevertheless, the author's and reader's responses are often ambiguous. But Lawrence, like Jung, lived in a period when positive approval of the Shadow seemed to some people a way of re-invigorating mankind. Accordingly, Cicio is intended to be commendable on the whole, though Alvina's feelings about him and what he represents are far from consistently admiring or worshipful.

What the fantasy-figure of Cicio meant to Lawrence is akin to what in other contexts he meant by snakes or serpents. In Lawrence's most anthologized poem, 'Snake', which was written in this period, the poet-narrator concludes that his feeling of shame over throwing a log at a snake is due to his recognition of the snake as 'one of the Lords of life'.

> For he seemed to me again like a king,
> Like a king in exile, uncrowned in the underworld,
> Now due to be crowned again.

The snake, which certainly represents the Freudian 'id', is less comprehensively the Jungian Shadow. (Jung repeatedly mentions snake-symbols in this connection.) It is 'due to be crowned again' because Christianity and, later, the rise of science, have held back and denigrated the beneficial forces that the snake represents. Cicio is also, in a manner of speaking, the snake, and *The Lost Girl* is one of Lawrence's attempts at releasing the snake-powers from bondage in the 'underworld'. But the snake—or Cicio—is only *one* of the lords of life; other lords of life, or dynamic psychic forces, are missing from the novel. In *Aaron's Rod* Lawrence tried, and explicitly failed, to bring about domination by his ego-consciousness; next, in *The Lost Girl*, he tried to bring about domination by his Shadow. He even pretended to have succeeded, for Alvina stays with Cicio, but subsequent novels belie the pretence.

Kangaroo, published three years later (1923), is more ambitious, psychologically speaking, because it brings into play a wider range of psychic forces. Once again, and more realistically than anywhere else, Lawrence included himself, as Richard Lovat Somers, and Frieda, in the person of Harriet. The novel contains—as so often in the later Lawrence—a curious combination, sometimes jarring but sometimes felicitous, of realism and fantasy. The 'real' Lawrences are there (and so, magnificently, is the real Australian scene), but they are brought into contact with not only a plausible political society, the 'Diggers', but also the less plausible political leader, Kangaroo. Kangaroo is another of Lawrence's fantasy-characters, partly at least representing forces within the author. Now, Lawrence's central difficulty at this period lies in the fact that he knows that his ego-consciousness (here depicted in the character of Somers) cannot properly subsist without a relationship to other aspects of his make-up, but he is still tending to assume that the relationship which he is seeking must be one of submission. He has experimented with submission to the 'higher' (Aaron to Lilly) and submission to the 'lower' (Alvina to Cicio); and now, as a further development, he tries out the notion of submission by the ego to a combination of the male and female principles, which, fully realized, would form the Jungian 'Self'. Kangaroo is an hermaphrodite figure whose appearance and manner crudely resemble a conjoined symbolic representation of the fundamental archetypes of Wise Old Man and Magna Mater. He has, or gives himself out to have, exactly the needed qualities of wisdom (including serpent wisdom) and relatedness to nature.

Kangaroo proposes that Somers should submit to his loving guardianship, and this Somers rejects. Furthermore, Lawrence contrives to have Kangaroo killed at a violent political meeting towards the end of the novel. In terms of Lawrence's development this is precisely as it should be, because Kangaroo is a premature and travestied version of the 'Self', or, viewed externally, of the individuated man. The love he offers is of the smothering variety, masking denial of individuality, which Lawrence always attributed to Christianity. The totally different state advocated by Jung, which I believe Lawrence was now urgently looking for, does not involve final authority or submission. In such a state the ego is neither exalted nor cast down; such alternatives as power or love cease to be alternatives, and dark gods become reconciled with light. It becomes clear that the following novel, *The Plumed Serpent*, was the obvious next stage in Lawrence's development.

Though *The Plumed Serpent* contains some very fine realistic scenes, such as the scenes of the bullfight and the attack on Jamiltepec, it is essentially a drama of inner forces, the main characters and events being embodiments of the author's most vital mental processes at this period of his life. It is not an allegory, but there is some advantage in viewing aspects of it as offshoots of the allegorical mode, for Lawrence projected his inward struggles in ways that can legitimately bring to mind, say, the medieval allegorists or Bunyan.

Lawrence largely kept his everyday, social self out of the novel and—apart from a few minor characters, such as Judge and Mrs Burlap—peopled it instead with fantasy-figures, who act out a drama remarkably reminiscent of Jung's process of individuation. Even Kate Leslie, the heroine, who owes a little to Frieda and who is given Lawrence's own mixed feelings of fascination, repulsion and wholesome scepticism, is basically another version of Lawrence's 'soul-image'. She lacks the idiosyncracies of the real Frieda (such as were previously portrayed in the character of Harriet Somers) and her central quest is the author's. Her second husband was an Irish intellectual who exhausted himself in political struggles, and now she longs for a new, more satisfying way of life. This is not Frieda, but the feminine segment of Lawrence, once again casting off the false leadership imposed by his own nagging, tormented post-war consciousness.

The Mexico that confronts Kate is, for all the graphic portraiture, also a country of the mind. What Kate initially finds in Mexico, in addition to the tawdriness of Mexico City, is a certain feeling of 'ponderousness'. The native soul is weighed down by the dragon of the Toltecs and Aztecs, which is to say that the natives suffer from an excess of unconsciousness. Kate has fled from European mentalism only to find herself amid an equally unwelcome barbarism. Revolted by Mexico City, she journeys to the interior, across Lake Sayula to the village of Sayula itself.

Kate's marvellous boat-trip over the lake reminds one in its tone and mood of some symbols of self-transformation, encountered principally in dreams, that Jung describes. Kate's journey is Lawrence's journey to the inner reaches of his mind. It is in and around

Sayula that Kate falls in with two remarkable men: Don Ramón Carrasco, who regards himself as the living representative of the god, Quetzalcoatl, and Don Cipriano, Ramón's warlike lieutenant. In the course of time, and with conflicting feelings, Kate joins these two, to form a triumvirate of disparate but interdependent figures.

Whatever the god, Quetzalcoatl, meant to the Aztecs and pre-Aztecs, Lawrence made of him a use of his own. The quetzal is the brilliantly-coloured Mexican bird; the word, 'coatl', means snake or serpent. Lawrence caused the bird half of his plumed-serpent god to represent the Spirit, while the snake, of course, represents the Flesh. These two aspects of human nature are also imaged by sky and earth, and by night and day. The Morning Star, which, appearing in the twilight, also can be said to unite night and day, is another image of reconciliation. The important fact to notice is that in these symbols though not consistently in the narrative, there is no question of superiority and inferiority, no question of submission. Ramón is a sufficiently credible figure of the individuated man for his hiero-phantic role to be acceptable to the reader. He can be acknowledged as in some sense a 'son of God'. Though he has troubles, political and domestic, he never seems to have much difficulty in relating these to the great natural process. His needs (for instance his need for his slavish second wife, Teresa) are not narrow, personal matters. But, of course, Ramón is an indigenous figure: indeed, it is part of the point of the novel that such a person could not readily be imagined in a European setting, though Lawrence at one point does postulate the desirability of a European equivalent of the Quetzalcoatl religion. What this amounts to is that Lawrence has come to see a goal very similar to Jung's, but has done so in the context of a fascinating, vividly realized, but alien country. Kate's indecision in the closing pages of the novel about staying in Mexico is due not chiefly to doubts about the Quetzalcoatl religion, but simply to the fact that she is not a Mexican.

If Lawrence has now glimpsed the Jungian goal of the 'Self', he has also, it seems, accepted Jung's means of reaching it, that is, by effecting an equal partnership between conscious and unconscious processes. Lawrence directs an action in which his 'soul-image', Kate, having also the conscious properties of scepticism, caution and perhaps downright perversity, is brought to a union with the Shadow-figure of Cipriano. Kate is Lawrence's feminine side, but she is also his commonsensical, 'upper' self, the finer and more comprehensive part of which is outside the story, performing the act of creation. Cipriano, black, instinctual, pure Indian, is the Shadow to whom she must be bound. Kate requires Cipriano, even as the 'white' European consciousness requires re-invigoration at its unconscious roots. Similarly, the Shadow-blackness of Cipriano would sink down into a kind of savage despair without a leavening of white consciousness. For these reasons Kate and Cipriano are 'married' in the rain; in other words as the sky, which is bird or Spirit, meets the earth, which is serpent or Flesh, in the form of life-giving moisture.

The Plumed Serpent is certainly a depiction of the individuation process, but it is also a dramatization of the extreme difficulties of that process. The novel is a mixture of apparent certainties and painful doubts. The ideals, summed up in Quetzalcoatl and the Morning Star, are asserted not hopefully or with bravado (as has so often been the case with other ideals in earlier novels) but with sureness. The Quetzalcoatl hymns, chants and rituals may make boring reading, but in them Lawrence seems more genuinely sure of his ground than he has been before. Here is no unwarrantedly optimistic vision of a rainbow, no Birkin struggling towards an incomplete conception, no Lilly pontificating to a reluctant Aaron: here instead for the first time is something approaching a fully realized vision of Being. The struggles given to Kate, when they are not connected with her sense of estrangement from home, are a pilgrim's struggles en route for an eternal city that the author knows is there and is almost sure he knows how to reach. But the journey entails terrors and Lawrence lacked a guide who could help him overcome them.

The Lawrences left Mexico for England because Lawrence fell seriously ill when completing *The Plumed Serpent*. His mixed feelings are recorded fictionally in 'The Flying Fish', and these feelings quite clearly arose from the desperate 'soul-adventure' that writing the novel constituted. Jung repeatedly asserts that the individuation process involves great perils and for this reason ought not to be attempted alone, without expert, sympathetic guidance. I believe that *The Plumed Serpent* is in part the expression of Lawrence's most determined effort to plumb the depths that Jung so often refers to, and towards the end of it he quite naturally grew afraid of the dangers to which he was heading.

He drew back completely from an abyss, which, theoretically, might also have proved to be an avenue of self-transcendence. The later fictions, whatever their literary merits and however interesting they might be, are not a forward development for Lawrence as a man. Despite the furore over *Lady Chatterley's Lover*, it is a less audacious book than *The Plumed Serpent*, because the attitudes that inform it are only modifications of comparatively 'safe' attitudes that Lawrence had held for years. The last story that Lawrence wrote, 'The Man Who Died', is impressive, because behind the now-familiar attempt to reconcile flesh and spirit and the concomitant assumption that Christianity subjugates the flesh, lies the awareness, beautifully treated, of the author's own approaching death. The death occurred, as it does for almost everyone, before what Jung saw as the goal of life had been reached.

Running alongside the works of fiction that I have discussed are many essays in which Lawrence more straightforwardly expresses views resembling Jung's. And in this fact lies an important point. When Lawrence wrote about such topics as the integration of the personality (to use Jung's phrase, not Lawrence's) in the generalizing manner which the essay-form demands, he inevitably failed to portray the extreme difficulties of what he was recommending. Naturally he mentioned or implied such difficulties, but that is not the same thing. Similarly, Jung regularly talks of 'perils' to the soul and refers to the intimate knowledge of these perils he has gained from contact with patients, but his works do not enable the reader to form more than a hazy impression of serious dangers. Because Jung was a thinker (and, of course, a practising physician) rather than an artist, he was able to build a system, which Lawrence, embroiled in the processes of creation, was unable and unwilling to do. But when they are both writing in general terms there are many points of agreement.

It was Lawrence who wrote: 'Never trust the teller, trust the tale.' In the essays he is simply a teller, and therefore, it seems, less trustworthy. One form the untrustworthiness takes is that the essays sometimes advocate ways of life that the novels show to be almost impossible. In 'Reflections on the Death of a Porcupine', for example, Lawrence writes:

Any creature that attains to its own fullness of being, its own *living* self, becomes unique, a non pareil. It has its place in the fourth dimension, the heaven of existence, and there it is perfect, it is beyond comparison.[9]

These words might very reasonably be taken as the best summary expression of what Lawrence, all his adult life, was driving at. They would also be appropriate as an epigraph to Jung's works. It should be noted that, apart from the obvious meaning, Lawrence, in italicizing the word, 'living', is stressing what Jung always stressed, namely the dynamic nature of the advocated condition. The 'heaven of existence' is not a stasis, but a process of ebb and flow, of continuous interaction. The point, however, is that Lawrence's words contain no hint of what the novels display: that is, the virtual impossibility of attaining to 'fullness of being'.

Similarly, in the essay, 'Democracy', Lawrence asserts:

The true identity, however, is the identity of the living self. . . . Every living creature is single in itself, a *ne plus ultra* of creative reality, *fons et origo* of creative manifestation.

Here is another encapsulation of Lawrence's fundamental message, but what he—like Jung—is talking about is a New Jerusalem, as hard to reach as the old.

It would be wrong to conclude these comments on similarities between Lawrence and Jung without stressing an important difference: that Lawrence was the practical explorer and Jung, for all his youthful difficulties, the theorist. Jung's system has a certain neatness, a roundedness which should probably arouse caution. On the other hand, Lawrence's response to life remained jagged and daring to the end.

4

THE SEARCH FOR IDENTITY

Proust, Virginia Woolf and the Neo-Freudians

Our record now begins to deal with a shift away from preoccupation with the unconscious instincts towards problems of personal identity. Some remarks of Marcel Proust offer a good starting-point.

On the 12th November, 1913 *Le Temps* featured an interview with Proust and included a copy of a statement written by him some time before, concerning his forthcoming novel, *A la Recherche du Temps Perdu*. Proust wrote in the statement:

> From this point of view, my book might be seen as an attempt at a series of 'novels of the unconscious'. I would not be ashamed to say 'Bergsonian novels' if I believed it, for in every age literature tries to find a link—after the fact of course—to the reigning philosophy. But the term would be inaccurate, for my work is based on a distinction between involuntary and voluntary memory, a distinction which not only does not appear in Mr Bergson's philosophy, but is even contradicted by it.[1]

Proust said that his entire vast work was *based* on a distinction between involuntary and voluntary memory, and most critics of Proust would agree with this. The distinction provided a foundation for the novel in two senses: first, it was an actual experience of involuntary memory that got Proust started on his novel, and secondly the justification of the novel is bound up with this rare form of recollection. What happened was that Proust one cold night in 1909 was given a cup of tea and some toast by his servant, and after he had dipped the toast into the tea he recalled with extraordinary vividness a garden in which he had played as a child. This of course was the basis of the famous 'madeleine' episode in *Swann's Way*, of which the narrator speaks as follows:

62

An exquisite pleasure had invaded my senses, but individual, detached, with no suggestion of its origin. And at once the vicissitudes of life had become indifferent to me, its disasters innocuous, its brevity illusory—this new sensation having had on me the effect which love has of filling me with a precious essence; or rather this essence was not in me, it was myself. I had ceased now to feel mediocre, accidental, mortal. Whence could it have come to me, this all-powerful joy? I was conscious that it was connected with the taste of tea and cake, but that it infinitely transcended those savours, could not, indeed, be of the same nature as theirs. Whence did it come? What did it signify? How could I seize upon and define it?[2]

Thus the narrator is invaded by an intense degree of what Freud called 'oceanic' feeling, an experience that has been variously described and valued down the ages. Proust's words are impressive in their down-to-earth precision: 'I had ceased now to feel mediocre, accidental, mortal.' The narrator's instant response is to question the feeling, not suspiciously or destructively, but at first out of sheer joyous curiosity and then laboriously. In the end, as the result of intense concentration, he recalls that when he was a child at Combray his aunt Léonie on Sunday mornings used to give him a portion of tea-soaked madeleine, and this simple recollection brings back the entire vista of Combray in the eighties: the garden, the river, the park, the church. Previously the narrator has forgotten these scenes and has remembered of Combray chiefly two floors of his childhood home and the hour of bedtime. If by an effort he had recalled other features of the town his mental pictures would have been influenced by subsequent experiences. The intellect, too, would have supervened and produced its own, false version of his early years; but now he remembers childhood as it actually was.

So ends the 'Overture' of *Swann's Way*, and immediately afterwards we move at slow pace via the details of the narrator's childhood and the personages he met or heard of towards the main stories of Swann's infatuation with Odette de Crécy and the narrator's love for Gilberte, Swann's daughter. But of course we have not finished with the business of involuntary memory, which is not just a device to start the novel, but also a philosophic groundwork. Certainly we hear very little more about involuntary memory until about half way through *Time Regained*, when almost all of importance in terms of plot has taken place. By this time the chief events and personalities have passed before us, of which the most prominent thread has been the narrator's relationship with Albertine. But Albertine has gone now, and other people with whom the narrator has been deeply involved, such as Saint-Loup and the Duchesse de Guermantes, or whom he has closely observed, such as the Baron de Charlus, have more or less lived out their seemingly pointless lives. Has there indeed been any point in the whole business, except the record of glitter and vanity and sadness and loss?

In fact Proust was, or became as a result of his experiences of involuntary memory, a philosopher, and not, I would argue, of the stoic sort. The vast record of Paris and 'Combray' and 'Balbec' from the eighties to the verge of the war was undertaken not to establish or lament over the vanity of human wishes, but to offset the futile round against reality. This is the purport of those passages in *Time Regained* generally seized upon by commentators.

For seventy pages of the last volume, beginning with Marcel's final visit to the Guermantes' mansion, Proust in effect explains what his novel has been about. As Marcel enters the courtyard he trips over some paving stones and then recalls a similar stumble over uneven stones in St Mark's cathedral in Venice. The miracle of involuntary memory has occurred again. A little later, while waiting in the sitting-room of the mansion, Marcel hears a servant chink a spoon against a plate, and this slight noise brings back to him the sound of a railwayman's hammer knocking against the wheel of a train halted in a wood. As a result of these two experiences, combined with the initial madeleine episode, the narrator is enabled to reach some general conclusions about time and personal identity. His lucid and profoundly interesting reflections are about both art and life. Literary critics are usually interested in the artistic doctrine, but in the following summary I shall concentrate on other aspects (though in fact the elements of the argument are not always completely separable).

The first point is familiar, for it concerns the jumbled nature of experience. A thought, a feeling, an action, whether trivial or important, rarely occurs in isolation but always as part of a context with which, however, it has little or no logical connection. The thought may have been produced by the context, but there are many features of the context that are extraneous to the thought. We seek to establish unity and significance by discarding such extraneous features, but in doing so we falsify the experience. So far Proust is a sort of phenomenologist, considering that descriptions of the moments of consciousness rather than analyses, summaries or abstractions are the nearest we can get to truth.

However, a context, in which is embedded some perception, is altered by our thoughts the very next moment. And so it continues being altered until, years later, its original character is quite forgotten. We believe that we have isolated and retained the perception, but this is impossible, since perception and context are part and parcel of each other. Memory seems to confer meaning and continuity upon our lives, providing us with a sense of identity, but since memories are distorted our self-images must be correspondingly inaccurate. Where then, if anywhere, can we find true identity? The dismaying answer would seem to be that we cannot find it, because it exists only in each moment of experience, and the moment cannot be grasped in all its purity. After an experience has taken place we form an image of it in an attempt to solidify it, to make it graspable, but the image is already impure. (Up to this point at least, whatever Proust's disavowals, his ideas are very like Bergson's.)

However, the pristine experience has been stored away within us, and magically returns through the workings of involuntary memory. When that happens there is no bridge, no obfuscating link between the present moment and a moment in the past. Proust's narrator now addresses himself to the obvious problem of why such an occurrence should seem valuable, or, rather, why it is certainly valuable, for, like all enjoyers of the mystical experience, he can entertain no doubt of its value. Nevertheless he seeks a rational explanation. The preliminary answer is that in a moment of involuntary memory the past is 'made to encroach upon the present', so the subject fleetingly exists outside time. He cannot be deluding himself, because he has discovered this extra-temporal dimension by accident, not through wishful thinking.

But the real explanation is yet to come. While the insight has been obtained through an extraordinary form of recollection, its implications cannot be confined to the operations of memory. Such an experience establishes beyond doubt that a mental image of a piece of reality can entirely correspond with one's sense impressions of that reality, and, furthermore, can subsist in the mind at one and the same time. Ordinarily this does not happen; what one imagines (has an image of) is not exactly what one perceives, has perceived or will perceive. And, to our deep regret, there is an 'ineluctable law which ordains that we can only imagine what is absent'.

I should make it clear that we are not talking about the difference between subjective and objective reality, between an object as it exists and the object as it appears to us. We are talking about two aspects of inner reality; between the sense-impressions of a thing and the image that we form of it. The image constitutes the attempt to confer meaning or coherence upon the sense-impression. We may attempt to form an image before, during, or after an experience. (The concoction of fantasy or fiction not related to an actual or expected experience is a complicating factor that can be left aside for the moment.) If we do so beforehand, the usual consequence is that reality differs from the daydream. Thus Marcel's dreams about Albertine are confounded by her lesbianism, and his assumptions about the grandeur of the Guermantes Way collide with the petty snobberies of real life. If we try to imagine an experience while it is taking place, the 'ineluctable law' to which Proust's narrator refers comes into operation, and the result is self-consciousness, diminution of the experience, anxiety. As a rule we cannot deliberately discover the meaning of an experience at the very moment of having it. Yet we must try to discover it, for we cannot move through, or for all practical purposes be, a succession of uninterpreted experiences. Hence the regular practice of forming an image after an experience, if the experience has been sufficiently stimulating.

This is to say that images before the event are a kind of trial run, while images after the event are a kind of re-run. In the former case we hope to fix the character of the event in advance (the business deal will be satisfactory or the surgeon's knife will not slip); in the latter we try to wrest significance from the welter of impressions. The ideal that we seek is a condition of complete coincidence between experience and image. We wish to enjoy and to contemplate at the same time; to exist and, without distancing ourselves, to know the manner of our existence. In a moment of involuntary memory this object is achieved, because, for instance, the image of Combray that came to the mature Marcel was only an image, and yet it precisely matched the sense-impression of childhood. A suitable succession of such moments would be the ideal psycho-analysis, the means to perfect self-understanding.

So runs a part of Proust's long argument. It will be seen that the argument amounts to a theory of personal identity, though Proust's own emphasis is on the nature of reality and of art rather than on the composition of consciousness. Of course it is a subjectivist theory, a complete reversal of the naturalists' beliefs that were prominent in France in Proust's boyhood. The individual's consciousness is thought of as consisting of an interaction between his sense-impressions and the images he forms of them. Integrity would seem to entail fidelity to one's impressions, and this in turn entails a mistrust of intellect. In fact Proust mounts an attack on the literature of ideas (descriptions of 'great working-class movements' or the 'Dreyfus affair'), on the grounds that a writer goes astray when he trades in ideas. He should have 'the strength to force himself to make an impression pass through all the successive states which will culminate in its fixation, its expression'. Presumably non-artists (as well as bad artists) are generally unable so to 'fix' their impressions, and therefore, if it were not for the ministrations of more talented people, would be condemned to live in an unreal, codified world.

Writing in this vein, Proust was giving body to ideas similar to those of Bergson, who postulated (prominently in *Time and Free Will*, but also to a degree in *Matter and Memory*) the fluidity of inner experience and the consequent impossibility of hardening such experience into the formulas of practical and social life. Later we shall notice the ways in which psychologists of the last twenty years have utilized the insights of Bergson and Proust, but first it will be profitable to consider the related attitudes of Virginia Woolf.

I intend to study in detail one of Virginia Woolf's preoccupations —indeed I would argue that it was her overriding preoccupation— and for this reason to focus attention on the one novel, *The Waves*, that includes few subsidiary concerns. The esoteric nature of *The Waves* is what makes it the perfect text from the point of view of this study. In writing other novels, especially from *Jacob's Room* onwards, Virginia Woolf pursued an understanding of the nature of identity, but in writing *The Waves* she drove clearly and without distractions as far as she could into the heart of the matter. In this sense, if in no other, it is the consummate Virginia Woolf novel.

There are seven characters in *The Waves*, called simply Rhoda, Jinny, Louis, Neville, Susan, Bernard, and Percival. The last of these is merely observed (with admiration) by the others, so that we know him only through their apprehensions of him. Intermittently he is the focus of the gaze of one or other of the six main characters, and continues to have this function after his death in India, which takes place mid-way through the novel. In other words, we are acquainted with Percival rather as we are acquainted with people in real life, when the relationship is not especially intimate. We know his gestures, his words, his actions; but we can only draw inferences about the quality of his inner experience. Percival has the coherence and opacity of any person seen from the outside. Similarly his death has the resonant effect of the death of any known, but not fully understood, individual. In life and death he is the Other, to the reader and to his fellow-characters.

But we come rapidly to know the six main characters at the very centre of each of them. Their looks, and even their actions, are relatively unimportant. The novel is a portrait of the *being* of each character. In her second novel, *Night and Day*, Virginia Woolf remarked that 'it's being and not doing that matters', and in her first novel, *The Voyage Out*, a character is given the ambition to write a novel 'about silence, the things people don't say'. The separation of being from doing is characteristic of Virginia Woolf (as of Proust), and it was in *The Waves* that she managed most thoroughly to relegate the world of action. Rhoda, Bernard and the rest simply *are*: their actions are comparatively unimportant manifestations of their inner states, whereas in life a good many actions are merely contingent or habitual. Even in the conventional novel (and almost all novels are conventional when set beside *The Waves*), while

67

actions tend to be expressive of character, they often assume importance in their own right. But in *The Waves* nothing matters but states of being.

Moreover these states are constant from the childhood of the characters until late middle age. The child is truly father of the man. Nobody changes or develops in any radical way. Though Rhoda commits suicide (most unobtrusively, as it happens) and though Bernard experiences a mystical vision at the end, these occurrences are consummations rather than departures. In Rhoda's beginning is her end; she was born to kill herself.

There is something in Virginia Woolf's view of the nature of consciousness that links her with two writers markedly different from her and from each other—Lawrence, whom we have considered, and Sartre, who will figure prominently in the next chapter. Lawrence talked of the 'spontaneous life-motive'; Sartre refers to the '*projet fondamental*'. As we have seen, Lawrence thought of attitudes and choices welling up from the 'true unconscious' of the individual, determining, if he will let them, his conduct and fate. Sartre's notion of the *projet* is a casting of oneself forward into the world in a certain chosen manner. One aims to be something, one projects oneself from nothingness towards being, though the target is never reached. The '*projet fondamental*' is an irreducible choice of one's nature, which may be made in the beginning, in infancy. Both Lawrence and Sartre regard such fundamental self-choices as subject to alteration, if the desire for alteration is strong enough. Here Virginia Woolf seems to differ, for her characters, once they have chosen a pattern for themselves, pursue it to the end. Just the same, a sort of self-determined core from which all the attitudes and actions spring is the unique feature of the characterization in *The Waves*.

Virginia Woolf evidently believed that each individual has such a core, but recognized that it is indescribable in ordinary terms. What then was her alternative to stopping short of the core and contenting herself with the established devices for depicting human consciousness? Her own earlier excursions into the minds of her characters had been adventurous enough. For instance, the reader of *Mrs Dalloway* forms a remarkably good idea of how Clarissa apprehends the world. But he still does not know precisely why Clarissa is so ready to adapt herself to the emotional requirements of others, to act as catalyst and mediator, to be the perfect hostess. Towards the end of the day of *Mrs Dalloway*, Clarissa, reflecting on the suicide of Septimus Warren-Smith, censures herself as follows:

She had once thrown a shilling into the Serpentine, never anything more. But he had flung it away. They went on living (she would have to go back; the rooms were still crowded; people kept on coming). They (all day she had been thinking of Bourton, of Peter, of Sally), they would grow old. A thing there was that mattered; a thing, wreathed about with chatter, defaced, obscured in her own life, let drop every day in corruption, lies, chatter. This he had preserved. Death was defiance. Death was an attempt to communicate, people feeling the impossibility of reaching the centre which, mystically, evaded them; closeness drew apart; rapture faded; one was alone. There was an embrace in death.[3]

Clarissa feels that inside her is a certain important 'thing' that she has allowed to spoil and waste away. Presumably she is thinking of what can only be called self hood, here imaged as a jewel, perhaps, embedded within herself, or as a treasure-chest or piece of statuary mouldering in a tangle of vegetation. Demeaning this 'thing' has given rise to regrets in Clarissa and a sense of security in the friends for whom, as an alternative to preserving her individuality, she has catered.

By the time of *The Waves* Virginia Woolf (having in the meantime explored an even more complete hostess in the person of Mrs Ramsay in *To the Lighthouse*) was apparently ready to tackle head-on the problem of the core of self hood. It is no longer a 'thing', in other words purely indescribable, but an image. Each character moves through *The Waves* bearing, as it were, an emblem that serves to define him or her.

The procedure is not too schematic, for that would probably be absurd, but from the early pages of the novel we begin to associate each character with the defining image. For Bernard it is a ring quivering in a loop of light; for Jinny, a crimson tassel twisted with gold thread; for Louis, a beast with its foot chained; for Susan, a slab of pale yellow; for Neville, a globe hanging down beside a hill; and for Rhoda, a frail bark sailing alone on treacherous seas. The six characters as small children tell us in their 'interior monologues' (the wrong phrase, but there is no other) that they see these images. Presumably we are to understand not that there is any actual picturing of a slab of pale yellow or a crimson tassel, but rather that these images function to express the sense of self and the self's relations with the world. Jinny, for instance, is not in the habit of picturing a crimson tassel twisted with gold threads, but she is already, as a pre-school child, a richly sensuous person for whom such an emblem is appropriate.

Within a few pages the basic stance of each character is established. We discover that Bernard is an explorer, imaginative, a seeker-out of new experiences for which he will delightedly find words. In adulthood he becomes a novelist. Jinny is a courtesan. Susan is maternal,

69

possessive, desiring security and roots. Neville loves to analyse and categorize, a scholar by nature. Louis (whose emblem is a great beast stamping) has an inferiority complex, in the full Adlerian sense, and therefore aims to triumph in the world: he becomes a money-maker. Rhoda is totally afraid, a frail vessel liable to be sucked down into the water. Paradoxically, her core is no core at all but an emptiness, so that as a child and as an adult she flounders about, trying in vain to become this or that, until in the end she kills herself.

There is a sense in which Bernard and Rhoda should be separated from the other four. Jinny, Susan, Neville and Louis each effect a partial adjustment to life. The natures with which they are endowed, or which Sartre would say they have chosen for themselves, are equipped to deal only with certain aspects of life. Jinny, for example (and this is made plain in the book), is going to have a hard time of it when her charms fade and sensual experience is impoverished. Likewise, Neville is uneasy and inefficient whenever circumstances do not permit the exercise of his powers of rational discrimination. (He is homosexual and suffers in his love affairs.) Susan is unhappy at school and is fulfilled only when she acquires a farmer-husband and children. Louis is at home buying and selling in the City, but bemused in intimate personal relationships. These four occupy mid-way positions on a scale, at opposite ends of which stand Bernard and Rhoda. Bernard's adjustment to life is very nearly perfect; Rhoda's is almost non-existent. Bernard has negative capability while Rhoda lacks all positive capabilities. He is no single thing because, imaginatively, he can be anything, whereas she feels herself to be simply nothing.

Virginia Woolf's contribution to our understanding of the human personality culminated in the composition of *The Waves*, and particularly in the portraits of Bernard and Rhoda. In bald summary we may express the contribution in the following way. Consciousness is fluid, amorphous; for survival it is necessary to attempt to confer a shape upon it, unless like Bernard, one can be protean. Any shape —Jinny's sensuality or Neville's intellectualism—is to some extent false, because consciousness cannot be crystallized. Jinny cannot be all sensuality; she merely refuses to widen her response to life. In other words she contracts herself into sensuality, because by so doing she can be a distinct person and avoid being swept away on the stream of impressions. Rhoda does not so contract herself, and therefore is swept away. She is unable to stand erect. Bernard is an embodiment of the most comprehensive solution. He actualizes not just one or two, but all his potentialities. He yields to the flow of experience without losing his grip upon himself. Like Edgar Allan Poe's fisherman in the story, 'A Descent into the Maelstrom', he survives by co-operating with the current. When the fishing smack in Poe's story is caught up in the vortex, this one seaman allows himself to be whirled around and around, lashed to a cask, while his brothers are destroyed by their frantic attempts to withstand the flow of water. This is a reasonable metaphor for Bernard's accommodation of the forces of life. At the end of the novel he is alone 'soliloquizing', having kept himself intact to a degree denied to the other five. Most interestingly, Bernard, like Proust's Marcel, experiences a vision of reality.

Bernard's vision is not initiated by a moment of involuntary memory. One day in old age he is leaning on a gate in the country when suddenly his train of thought stops. His mind becomes empty, the state people aim for when they practise meditation. He loses all sense of self. He sees the fields before him, but cannot think about them, or about himself, or indeed about anything. He feels that he has been destroyed. Then the rural scene changes character, growing colourless and devitalized, as if some vast blight has descended. In total despondency Bernard allows his weight to push open the gate, and shortly afterwards colour and fertility return to the landscape. But the scene is incomparably richer than it was before, for Bernard is seeing it as if he himself were not there. No thoughts, no intentions or other distractions interpose the usual muddy filter between perceiver and perceived. 'So the landscape returned to me', Bernard recollects; 'so I saw fields rolling in waves of colour beneath me, but now with this difference; I saw but was not seen. I walked unshadowed; I came unheralded. From me had dropped the old cloak, the old response; the hollowed hand that beats back sounds.'[4]

The cloak, the response, the hollowed hand are ways of picturing the hardened sense of self with which even Bernard, for all his malleability, has hitherto confronted the world. This is not the ego exactly in Freud's sense, nor yet the ego in the popular sense of self-regard; but rather the usual, more or less inescapable sense of oneself as a distinct thing. Virginia Woolf in drawing her portraits of the characters in *The Waves* illustrated a paradox of the human condition: the sense of self is a fabrication that preserves the individual while veiling reality. This is approximately what T. S. Eliot meant when, after describing a moment 'out of time' in 'Burnt Norton', he wrote, 'Human Kind cannot bear very much reality.' In Virginia Woolf's novel no one can bear very much reality, but Bernard can tolerate at least a few moments of it. His capacity must be the product of extraordinary self-confidence, so that he allows himself to split into fragments, knowing that the fragments will cohere again. More precisely, the fragments are different selves over which some factor in Bernard can exercise control. Virginia Woolf had previously glanced at such a factor when, in *Orlando*, she had spoken of 'the Key self, which amalgamates and controls them all'.[5]

We are now in a position to note some similarities between Virginia Woolf's vision and Proust's. (She in fact began reading Proust in 1922 and was rather miserable on discovering how well he had managed something akin to what she was attempting.[6]) Both Marcel and Bernard are artists capable of empathy, and each enjoys a mystic experience. Marcel's insight is to the effect that reality consists in a perfect coincidence between an image and the sense-impression of which it is the image. Bernard's understanding comes through glimpsing the world without a sense of self. The two insights, though differently expressed, amount to the same thing. In each instance impressions of the world 'out there' (the vista of Combray or Bernard's landscape) would normally be distorted by desires and fears, by preconceptions, by any of the forms of self-concern. The 'image' of which Proust speaks is, in its regular corrupt form, composed of such elements; the crystallized consciousness exemplified in Virginia Woolf's characters is both cause and consequence of such corrupt images. Liberation comes through purification of the image, which, when complete, must be the equivalent of an abnegation of self. Of course the purified image is still one's own image: it does not possess some mechanical objectivity, like the objectivity of a photograph. The self that is abnegated is not the real personality, but rather the false or partial personality with which one regularly confronts the world.

In this way, working introspectively and in terms of natural psychology, Proust and Virginia Woolf arrived at a modern version of something that down the ages has been interpreted in religious terms. Certain psychologists working later than these two novelists have come to comparable conclusions. Most of these psychologists are classified as neo-Freudians or post-Freudians, though some existential psychologists who owe little to Freud have produced similar ideas.

Roughly speaking, the neo-Freudians have been concerned with relations between the ego and the outside world rather than with the power and proclivities of the instincts. They have not discarded the concept of the unconscious, but, like Freud himself in his later years, focus little attention upon it.[7] This means of course that they have explored the same territory as Virginia Woolf and Proust. The same question underlies their work: what constitutes the self? What must a person do to have complete self-possession? Alternatively, how is it that some individuals (such as Virginia Woolf's Rhoda and Septimus Warren-Smith) have so little sense of identity?

An answer was attempted by Anna Freud, the first post-Freudian whose work we should consider, in *The Ego and the Mechanisms of Defence* (1937). The implication of this short book is that the ego is best preserved by an absence of defences. In other words, the ego, which is so vulnerable in childhood, can be strengthened only by continual contact with reality. Any form of armour or shell keeps the weak little self in a state of dependency. Freud of course held the same attitude, and one is reminded of George Eliot's advice, in a pre-psychoanalytical age, to live without 'opiates'. And to Anna Freud, as to Virginia Woolf (whose Hogarth Press published *The Ego and the Mechanisms of Defence*), consciousness means the entirety of one's more valuable perceptions, not just bits hived off for comfort. One might reasonably say that Virginia Woolf's Bernard is a person with a minimum of defence-mechanisms.

Anna Freud's book largely consists of a description of several ways of defending the ego, each of which entails a falsification of what the person has actually experienced. He may deny the truth, either in fantasy or in 'word and act'; he may restrict the ego; he may identify himself with whatever is feared, or he may seek vicarious satisfactions. Denying the truth means simply pretending that something unpleasant is pleasant, and one often does this by means of fantasy. Alternatively one may inwardly call the unpleasant experience by some pleasant name, or behave as though the pleasant interpretation were correct. These devices are too well recognized to need amplification. The next defence-mechanism, restriction of the ego, is barely recognized at all and seems to correspond to what we have noticed in four of the characters in *The Waves*. Anna Freud offers the example of a young girl who cultivates her intellectuality in compensation for social failure. The full implications of such behaviour are not pursued in Anna Freud's book, but to do so leads to an assessment of human personality along the lines of Virginia Woolf's novel. Neville, for instance, shrinks away from intimate personal relationships into a world of scholarship. By the time we meet Neville he, like all the characters, has already arrived at his adjustment to life. But where did the process begin? Presumably Neville was not born with a scholarly temperament; presumably no one is. At some stage in his infancy he opted for rational thought as a means of warding off discomfort. We cannot say that such discomfort in spheres other than the intellectual indicates congenital intellectuality, for it is more likely that Neville in his very early life had various alternatives open to him. In this connection it is instructive to read Sartre's autobiography, *Words*, which, as the title suggests, shows how one young intellectual unconsciously strengthened his verbal abilities in order to control the painful confusion of his experiences.[8] Restriction of the ego seems in some degree to be almost a universal defence-mechanism: only the Bernards and Rhodas of this world escape it completely.

Similarly, there is a widespread tendency to identify with a feared object or person, a procedure that psychologists call 'introjection'. At a superficial level—laughing at the boss's witless joke for instance —the practice of camouflaging oneself is well understood, but Anna Freud discusses less deliberate self-identifications. Here again, *The Waves* offers a striking commentary and a deeper penetration into the subject. Rhoda, who fears everybody, identifies with everybody. She copies other people's gestures, not simply to learn through imitation, but to avoid being the wrong kind of person. And she is always the wrong kind of person because she is not someone else. Clearly, on Anna Freud's kind of analysis, she cannot toughen her ego until she stops trying to defend it; that is, until she takes the fearful risk of being herself. But what self? By the time we meet her she has been 'introjecting' for so long that any attempt to be herself would be limited to another piece of panicky role-playing.

Later psychologists than Anna Freud (not all of whom would regard themselves as Freudians) have followed the same path. It has become common to talk of 'exteriorization of the object' and of 'mature object relations', which rather uncouth phrases sum up a theory about the process of maturing. It is held that the new-born baby cannot distinguish between himself and the rest of the world. Presumably the baby 'knows' in some obscure way that an object, including a part of his own body, is apart from his subject-awareness of it, but the feelings he has towards the object (and his awareness is purely emotional) are attributed to the object. In particular objects are 'good' or 'bad', according to whether they give him pleasure or pain; and the same object (for example, the mother's breast) may be good or bad depending on the circumstances. It is easy to compare this account of the infantile nature with ordinary manifestations of childishness in adults, as for instance when an adult regards a person who displeases him as bad, despite that person's reasonable intentions. It is also easy to see that a fully mature person, on this theory, is one who is fully alive to the otherness of others. The mature individual has little tendency either to 'introject' other people's qualities into himself or to 'project' his own qualities on to others. Virginia Woolf's Bernard is such a person: in complete security he can flow in and out of the minds of friends, precisely because he knows, has trained himself from childhood to know, that they are apart from himself. The zenith of his maturity is reached when, for a few minutes in old age, he sees a landscape as something quite distinct from his own thoughts and feelings. Conversely Rhoda is never liberated from confusion between herself and others. They are liable to swallow her up. Even more plainly is this so with Septimus Warren-Smith in *Mrs Dalloway*; his madness consists of a regular feeling that he is being incorporated into the world around him.

The views I have just been outlining are in small measure those of Melanie Klein but mainly those of the British psychologist, W. R. D. Fairbairn, whose book, *Psychoanalytic Studies of the Personality* (1952), has been very influential, especially in the United States. However, I have only glanced at some features of Fairbairn's ideas, which constitute a depth psychology, and therefore go beyond what a novelist could represent. His theory postulates one fundamental pathological condition, the schizoid (from which everyone suffers to a greater or lesser extent), though a variant of this condition, the depressive attitude, arises in some people. Schizoid and depressive tendencies originate in the infant's relations with its mother. But the novelist, even Virginia Woolf in *The Waves*, must start at a later stage in the development of her characters, when the dispositions have become relatively fixed.

Nevertheless, in dealing with the dispositions of his characters a novelist works on a set of assumptions, and such assumptions sometimes rise to the level of a full-blown theory. Not surprisingly theories held by novelists tend to be *en rapport* with the reigning philosophy (as Proust remarked). In the earlier years of this century philosophic and literary notions of human personality were often, as we have noted in previous chapters, biological and individualistic. Freud's was an individual psychology rooted in biology. Jung and Adler (in his early days) were also individual, as opposed to social, psychologists. Jung was never much interested in the biological foundations of human nature but was deeply concerned with cultural history, while Adler's theories rested to some extent upon an analogy between psychological and physiological mechanisms of compensation. Bergson, who lies behind Proust and Virginia Woolf, studied the individual's relations with others but not the individual's relations with society at large. It is fair to say that up to the 1930s both psychologists and novelists tended to view the social world as a product of individual psychology and of biological forces in man (the instincts), whereas since that time there has been greater emphasis on the individual as a product of social forms. Thus we are all now aware of the debate between those who believe that aggression is a primary instinct and those who argue that aggression is merely the result of faulty social arrangements.

The central question we are now concerned with, the question of personal identity, prominently entails consideration of how far the individual is determined by either social or instinctual forces. Proust and Virginia Woolf attached little importance to such considerations: to both of them the social world was simply the environment with which their characters had to cope. This is a commonsensical view, for while it is obvious that a Clarissa Dalloway or a Duchesse de Guermantes would be a different person if transported at an early age to a totally different environment, the interesting problem is why each character is precisely what she is and not something else. Mayfair and Bourton have not made Clarissa so much as limited her possibilities; but the range of possibilities, at all events in her early life, was still very wide.

But what of the instincts, that is, of the unconscious in Freud's sense? Virginia Woolf in *To the Lighthouse* certainly rested the nature of the boy, James Ramsay, upon oedipal foundations, and in the 'Time Passes' section of that novel represented the unconscious by portraying cosmic tumult, the universe unordered by mind. Quite often in Virginia Woolf the individual unconscious is *externalized*: it is manifested in the significance that she, rather than her characters, confers upon external objects. Nevertheless her focus is on the 'upper' sense of identity of the characters in their overt dealings with one another.

Proust and the neo-Freudian psychologists even more thoroughly laid aside the concept of the unconscious. Proust, admittedly, in the statement printed by *Le Temps* talked of a series of 'novels of the unconscious', but he clearly meant the Bergsonian rather than the Freudian unconscious. He meant not a seething mass of unknowable instincts, nor even the 'spontaneous life-motive' of Lawrence, but just those processes of the mind that we find almost impossible to observe because of their amorphousness. Sometimes what Proust means by the unconscious is scarcely the unconscious at all, but only a set of impressions that for some reason the individual ignores. Marcel forgets almost all his childhood impressions of Combray because, so it seems, he chose to put a certain, false interpretation on his childhood. This may be a species of repression, but it is far from the psycho-analysts' repression, because the forgotten experiences were in fact happy ones.

As it happens a particular post-Freudian (rather than neo-Freudian) psychologist has stressed this kind of psychic manoeuvre. The American, Harry Stack Sullivan, in his *Conceptions of Modern Psychiatry* (1947), postulates an unconscious that is the result of 'selective inattention', in other words that is similar to, but not the equivalent of, Freud's 'preconscious'. According to Sullivan's theory the individual in childhood pays attention chiefly to the elements in his experience that arouse least anxiety, or only the most controllable types of anxiety. In this way as time goes by he becomes a certain sort of a person: he limits himself, just as, according to my conjecture, several characters in *The Waves* have limited themselves by the time the novel begins.

Such post-Freudian theories as those of Anna Freud, Fairbairn and Sullivan have in common the belief that character, or personality, is a kind of shape hewn out of larger and rougher material. This material may or may not include the Freudian unconscious (Anna

Freud thought that it did; Sullivan thought that it did not), but in either case there is the assumption that the individual could have developed a different shape, a different character, from the one he now has. To begin with he is mainly shapeless raw material, though he has inherited limitations of physique, nervous system and possibly other elements such as level of intelligence. Then, imperceptibly but rapidly in infancy, he, the tiny self-sculptor, selects the elements in his variegated experiences to which he wishes to pay attention, and the sort of response—aggressive, submissive, emotional, reflective etc.—that he finds it least painful to make. Thus the original material is cut down, refined and hardened into a distinct form. None of these three psychologists explicitly says anything quite like this, but it is a reasonable inference from the tenor of their work.

In such a way a sense of identity is acquired; a strong sense in some individuals, a weak sense in others. But at this point, assuming the soundness of the general theory, at least two very interesting questions remain. First, is it preferable for the infant to assume as variable an identity as he can without losing control of himself, or is it, on the contrary better for him to cultivate a hard, fixed mould? Proust, Virginia Woolf, and the neo-Freudians seem to have favoured the first course. In poets and other creative workers this variability is manifested as 'negative capability', while in persons with less recognized talents it presumably still gives rise to wide powers of empathy. Such people do not, for example, confront the world in a predominantly emotional or a predominantly rational way; they do not develop lopsidedly. This is what may be termed the 'Odysseus' nature in contrast to the 'Achilles' nature. Odysseus' supreme adaptability (which included, but was not composed of, wiliness) was the opposite of Achilles' incapacity to be other than martial, arrogant and self-willed. But would anyone say that Achilles had the more integrated personality? The Achilles way is sometimes spoken of with approval by Lawrence who admired (though he did not necessarily like) individuals who are distinct, special, unaccommodating. Cultivate, not one's garden, but one's distinctiveness. This is the way of the 'egotistical sublime'. To offer one small example, Lawrence, in the 'Study of Thomas Hardy', speaks approvingly of Sue Bridehead as having a 'being, special and beautiful'. He asks, 'Why must it be assumed that Sue is an "ordinary woman"—as if such a thing existed? Why must she feel ashamed if she is specialised?'[9]

The second interesting question is whether or not the choices made by the child are in any acceptable sense choices at all. We are left with the old opposition between free will and determinism.

Both of these problems can be pursued further in relation to developments in twentieth-century literature and psychology only by considering the next phase, the phase of existentialism.

5

ATTACK ON THE
UNCONSCIOUS

Sartre and the Post-War American Novel

Proust's description of *A la Recherche du Temps Perdu* as 'an attempt at a series of "novels of the unconscious" ' did not mislead us into supposing that he meant anything resembling the psycho-analysts' unconscious. He meant instead what Bergson called the 'fundamental self', which lies beneath the 'social self'. This philosopher did not speak of the unconscious but of two forms of consciousness: the first, utilitarian, a fabricator of symbols and concepts; the second, 'confused, ever changing and inexpressible'.[1]

Inexpressible, but not unknowable, for an aware person can sense the shapeless processes of this second level of consciousness in his own mind. But what has happened to the Freudian concept of the unconscious, which is by definition unknowable? Somehow in our survey as in the development of thought after the 1920s, this concept has been left behind, or aside. Freud himself began to shift his attention away from the unconscious at about that time, and the post-Freudians, starting with Anna Freud in the thirties, concentrated, as we have noted, on the processes of the ego. Still the notion of the unconscious had not been disposed of, but merely assimilated—by many psychologists, novelists and the public at large. Possibly such assimilation was premature, for hostile critics, at least, regarded it as a hypothesis, not a proven fact, like evolution. The psycho-analysts themselves maintained that it had been validated, in the same way that all hypotheses must be validated, by observation and experiment. It had been shown again and again, they said, that people did repress memories of unpleasant experiences and that such experiences could be recalled by appropriate means. Since these repressed experiences continued to have an effect on the person's behaviour they must have been lodged somewhere in the meantime, and this somewhere could only be called the unconscious. Arguments against the existence of the unconscious used to come mainly from behaviourist psychologists or from some positivist philosophers and were therefore not taken to heart. When you are attacked by the official opposition you tend to make at most tactical revisions, not changes of basic doctrine.

Lawrence's attack, which we considered in an earlier chapter, was of an 'informed' nature and therefore should have been taken seriously. One might say that Lawrence was on the side of the angels because he believed that people are psychically determined and that their most forceful motivations are unconscious. The real opposition was not Lawrence but the mechanists, those who saw human beings as responding more or less predictably to external stimuli. Lawrence, anyway, did not deny the existence of the Freudian unconscious: he merely argued that such an unconscious was not unconscious enough. It was a 'shadow cast from the mind', whereas the true unconscious was prior to mind. The true unconscious was possessed even by relatively mindless animals and consisted partly of pure instincts and partly of self-determining impulses.

In fact Lawrence, as I have briefly noted,[2] was wrong in supposing the Freudian unconscious to be entirely composed of repressed material. Concomitantly he seems to have been ignorant of Freud's belief that unconscious processes fundamentally shade off into somatic activities. However, leaving aside these qualifications, it will be seen that the most important difference between Lawrence and Freud has to do with the question of determinism. Both believed that a man's essential self is determined from outside the conscious processes. But to Freud this was a regrettable condition to be remedied by increased understanding of unconscious drives. Gradually the ego would take control of the id, as a rider tames a horse: the power of the horse remains but is intelligently and profitably directed. To Lawrence, on the other hand, the true unconscious must be left to itself, for it has intelligence and a sense of direction of its own, far superior to anything the ego can think up. Thus Lawrence firmly anchored the ego to the biological world, while Freud, who also believed in a biological basis for man's behaviour, hoped that man would eventually dominate that basis through scientific knowledge. In Lawrence, though there are many polarities, there is no fundamental dualism: man and nature, body and mind, are one. But in Freud there is, in an emphatic form, the inevitable subject-object dichotomy of science.

The next stage in the development of twentieth-century concepts of being is part—a central part—of the growth of existentialism. So far as novelists and psychologists were concerned this was an unobtrusive growth in the twenties and thirties because the work of the leading existentialist thinkers, Jaspers, Husserl and Heidegger, was not widely disseminated at that time. The early work of Jaspers and Husserl was published in German in 1913, and Heidegger's *Being and Time* was first published, also in German, in 1927, but widespread interest in these philosophers began to develop only in the forties and fifties. And of course it was through Sartre and other French existentialists that the older German existentialists became accessible.

This would not have happened, I suppose, or would have happened to a lesser extent, if Sartre had not been primarily a professional writer. The existentialist philosophers can be viewed—and often contemptuously are viewed—as mere amateur psychologists. Sartre is the worst of the lot from this scholastic standpoint because he is a literary artist as well as an amateur psychologist. This means that while calling himself a philosopher he has contributed influentially to a science in which he has received no training, and has often done so in rhetorical rather than scientific language.[3] But of course it is Sartre's audacity in confusing literature, psychology and philosophy that makes him so important a figure for our purposes.

Sartre's later work in the 1960s aims at a 'totalizing' picture of man and therefore embraces not only the 'disciplines' that I have mentioned but every relevant field of study, prominently including history, sociology and political theory. However, we must concentrate on the less heterodox mixture of philosophy and psychology that is *Being and Nothingness*.

In Chapter Two of the Introduction to this work is Sartre's famous refutation of Freud's (and, by implication, Jung's) notion of the unconscious. The refutation is total, as it must be since the unconscious is incompatible with that freedom of the will that it is the central object of *Being and Nothingness* to establish.

The unconscious is replaced in Sartre's scheme by 'bad faith,' which means the retention in the mind of mutually incompatible ideas. A few moments of honest thought would reveal to the individual that if one of the ideas is true, the other must be false, but it brings comfort to entertain both. Bad faith is self-deception, but it is more fundamental and more widespread than the type of activity we commonly designate as self-deception. Most people, in Sartre's view, are in bad faith most of the time, because they fail to recognize how free and how responsible for themselves they are. If a woman is frigid it is because she chooses so to be; if a man is paralyzed with fear this is intentional on his part. Even our emotions are chosen, Sartre conjectures in *Sketch for a Theory of the Emotions* (1939). Clearly the choices do not arise from deliberation: in fact they, or an awareness of their consequences, arrive spontaneously, in full consciousness. Any antecedent 'thoughts' were, and probably still are, preconscious rather than unconscious. Thus the woman's frigidity was chosen preconsciously and her responsibility would become clear to her if she shifted her gaze. Obviously her will is set against the recognition of her own devices but it is theoretically, and sometimes practically, possible for her to recognize them. On the other hand, repressed material in the unconscious proper is inaccessible except by means of a full-scale analysis. So far in making these assertions Sartre, it seems to me, is pushing downwards the frontier of the unconscious rather than disposing of it altogether. He is not, for example, taking account of originating experiences (real or imagined) in infancy, except by implying that the infant's way of dealing with those experiences constituted a blind, self-defining 'choice'.

Sartre tilts against the belief that has been held down the centuries, and of which Freud's is only a modern form, that the individual is impelled by forces external to the conscious processes. Once it was thought that a human being could be impregnated by evil spirits; now it is still common to suppose that one can be governed by emotions that are automatically triggered off by some event. Sartre, I think, would equate the ancient and modern beliefs. The modern man who considers that his feelings invade him, dictating his behaviour, exhibits no great advance on a person in the seventeenth century imagining that an emissary of the devil has produced his anger or his lust.

Sartre's contention is that the psyche is one and indivisible. Freud's scheme, he argues, splits the psyche into two parts, an ego which is me, and an id which in some curious fashion is not me. Thus 'I' can be motivated by wishes that are not truly 'me', because they are in the unconscious. I am the ego, but I am not the id. The id is composed of forces that simply exist, beyond good and evil, beyond truth and falsehood. It is therefore not to be equated with the devil, pure evil, but it has the same function in robbing the individual of complete responsibility for his actions and character.

Furthermore, a person who wishes to know himself (because, for instance, he has developed neurotic symptoms) must apply to an analyst who will then proceed to act as mediator between the person's ego and id. This means, says Sartre, that one can know oneself only through the good offices of another. This other will sooner or later explain one's id to one's ego. Still however, the id is separate; it remains the object to be known by the subject, the ego.

But before this increase in self-knowledge is produced there invariably occurs the phenomenon of resistance. As the analyst's probings approach the truth, the analysand offers resistance. Or rather, that is how the proceedings are usually explained, leaving open the question of who precisely does the resisting. The patient is not one, but two people, ego and id. If it is his ego that resists, how does the ego know when the dreaded truth is about to be uncovered? On the other hand the id is scarcely likely to resist the analyst's questioning, because the id has all along sought to elude the censor, to reach the light of day, to express itself.

The answer given by psycho-analysis is that it is this mechanism called the censor that puts up the resistance. Now the censor must be a component either of the ego or of the id. If it belongs to the ego, it must know what the buried impulses are and why they should remain buried. If on the contrary, it belongs to the id, it cannot know what they are and therefore cannot know when to steel itself against the interrogation.

What Sartre does not specifically say, but clearly believes, is that the so-called censor is part of the so-called ego; therefore, whenever a person squirms before the questions of his analyst it is because he —*he* as a whole person not as a differentiated ego—knows quite well what it is that he is reluctant to have brought to the forefront of his mind. We can assume that Sartre believes that a patient suffering from hysterical paralysis, for example, knows in some obscure way that the paralysis is deliberate and even why she is behaving in this fashion. In the immediately relevant section of *Being and Nothingness* Sartre does not discuss actual or imagined cases of this sort, but merely quotes the psychiatrist Stekel as saying: 'Every time that I have been able to carry my investigations far enough, I have established that the crux of the psychosis was conscious.'[4] The implication is of course that if even the crux of a psychosis (an insanity) is conscious, then the same is plainly true of less irrational conditions, from neurosis to normality. There is no unconscious, at least in Freud's sense of the word. Proponents of psycho-analysis, says Sartre, have conferred upon the devices of self-deception the status of a respectable objective mechanism: they have 'reified bad faith'.[5]

It is clear that this line of argument leads us to a conception of the human individual as integrated and purposeful. His psyche is one conscious whole. There are no complexes, in the strict sense of bits of the personality split off from the rest and operating more or less independently. A neurosis is not 'in' a person, on the model of a virus or some other debilitating invader: it is an expression of the entire personality. R. D. Laing, the best-known existential psychologist in Britain, rams this point home by quoting from Hopkins's sonnet, 'I am gall, I am heartburn', and remarking that Hopkins knew that this condition was *him*. 'Thousands of people', Laing ironically points out, 'have come to psychiatrists to be "cured" of less than this.'[6]

Towards the end of *Being and Nothingness* Sartre provides a conspectus for an existential psycho-analysis. The initial assumption is that 'human reality' is defined by ends, by desires. (This assumption is faintly reminiscent of Adler's individual psychology and also of Lawrence's 'spontaneous life-motive', but Sartre's picture is more all-embracing than Adler's and eschews the cosmic connections that Lawrence postulates.) Sartre contends that desires are not in oneself, but are oneself. He illustrates this by reference to a common form of biographical writing in which the subject's future achievements are supposedly explained by various elements of his childhood. He maintains that such explanations explain nothing, for they never take into account the alternative paths that the subject, in consequence of his early experiences, might have followed. Thus Flaubert cannot be said to have become a writer as a means of symbolically satisfying a need for violence and intensity (as one biographer has alleged), for on the evidence given he might just as well have grown into an actor or a musician. Flaubert became a writer simply because at some moment he decided to take up writing: our enquiries cannot get beyond that point. The salient fact is that nothing external to the young Flaubert's will caused him to become a writer. More precisely, since the will of Flaubert and the personality of Flaubert were in all important respects the same thing, all we can say is that Flaubert opted for writing.

This might not be difficult to accept in respect of a vocation such as authorship, but of course Sartre applies the same argument to character. Why was Flaubert ambitious? For no reason other than that he chose this way of dealing with the world. Later on, in *Saint Genet*, Sartre asserts that Jean Genet followed a career of vagrancy and crime as a result of the discovery in childhood that he was an object, designated 'thief', to others. Thus he interiorized a certain objectification of himself. But his writings consisted of a conquest of his fate through a process of exteriorizing this object-self. Thus while we are limited by other people, by social forms and by history, there is always the possibility of transcending these limitations. It will be seen that Sartre's view of freedom resembles Hegel's notion of the recognition of necessity and Nietzsche's of loving one's fate.

According to Sartre all our mistaken notions about the nature of being spring from one basic error, the error of idealism. We tend to take it for granted that people, like artefacts, have a kind of pre-existent essence; that they are something in theory before they do anything in practice. And what they do in practice, according to this erroneous belief, is only a partial or accidental or misconceived manifestation of the invisible essence. Therefore, Sartre argues, the notion of potentiality is often falsely applied to human character and deeds. A man is defined by his actions and to believe that he might have behaved otherwise is sometimes consolatory and always idle. 'Why should we attribute to Racine the capacity to write yet another tragedy when that is precisely what he did not write?'[7] We cannot be more or less than what we do because, presumably (though Sartre does not say so), capacities are not separable from one another or from the whole man and the direction of his life in specific circumstances. To say that Jude Fawley could have produced a fine work of scholarship is to separate artifically his aptitude for study from his other propensities. More precisely, the error here is to think of aptitudes as if they existed independently of doings. Proust was not first possessed of some mysterious quality called 'genius', which compelled or enabled him to write certain books. The genius of Proust resides in and only in his productions. Sartre applies a similar argument to the might-have-beens of history. The Second World War was not historically determined, that is produced by economic and social forces acting independently of man's desires. In fact young Germans apprehended the Treaty of Versailles as a humiliation and developed a desire for revenge, whereas young Frenchmen saw the Treaty as a victory and wished for continuing peace. The will of the German people was, as it happened, stronger. It is vain to speculate that the relative strength of these wills could have been reversed.

The Sartrean position is that a man is not to be defined in terms of the general tendencies of his past behaviour, but in terms of what he wills for the future. At any given moment he is non-being willing himself towards being. If he allows his present actions to be dictated by the tendencies of the past (by habit), that is merely a choice not a necessity. He cannot truthfully say. 'I am incorrigibly what I have become', but only that 'I do not choose to change.' All one's thoughts are directed towards the future, so that if one 'dwells in the past' it is perhaps for the purpose of not changing in the future, or possibly in order to discover for future use some secret of happiness that one seemed in the past to possess.

Moreover, each action, mental or physical, is an attempt at self-realization, at constituting oneself as a solid being. The example that Sartre selects in *Being and Nothingness* is that of a straightforward physical activity: rowing. If I observe of a man that he likes to go rowing I would probably not regard this liking as an insignificant fact. Nor should I so regard it, for the rowing certainly points to something beyond itself. However, under the influence of traditional beliefs I would be likely to make the mistake of assuming that the rowing was an expression of the man's character. The error here lies in attributing to the man a prior nature independent of the rowing, of which the rowing is a sort of fortuitous outgrowth. The converse error to this one is to suppose that by making a list of the man's chosen activities I could arrive at a definition of his total being. On this assumption, which Sartre says is commonly found in novelists, a human being is the sum or essence of his doings. But such a sum or essence does not exist; it is a pure abstraction.

So here is the problem: if a man does not possess an inherent nature of which his activities are an expression, and if, on the other hand, we cannot deduce his nature by aggregating his activities, how then can we attribute being to him? Is he not just a meaningless sequence of doings? (Kafka, above all other novelists, sees man in this way. More precisely, most of the characters in Kafka's tales are a meaningless sequence of doings, though they fail to recognize the fact, while the heroes are heroes because they cannot bear the meaninglessness.)

Sartre's answer is that man is indeed nothing in himself. Therefore, insofar as he is anything at all, he is what he does; for example, he is a rower. But the rowing is not just rowing: it is an attempt to confer meaning on the world. However, while the man is a rower, he is obviously not a rower in the sense that the boat is a boat. As a matter of fact the man is a nothingness-in-himself who aspires to be something-in-himself, and his meaning lies in his lack and his aspiration. Since this consummation can never be achieved, 'man is a useless passion'. (*L' homme est une passion inutile.*)

Sartre distinguishes three regular forms of consciousness, three categories of psychic process. The first of these is the 'pre-reflective *cogito*', which is simply the normal condition of the mind when one is more or less concentrating on what one is doing. In this condition the attention is fixed on the outside world or on one's activity (which may be no more strenuous than daydreaming or lazing in the sun), but there is a vague, implicit awareness of oneself. The second form is denominated 'being-for-others', and this means self-consciousness in the popular sense. The individual is aware of himself as an object to others: he sees himself as they see him, or as he imagines they see him. He is a specimen, classified and unalterable. He is sociable, or bookish; he is a model child or he is naughty: his character and fate are what he believes others deem them to be. ('And how should I presume?' asks T. S. Eliot's Prufrock, meaning, how can I presume to upset others' convictions about me and about my relationships to these others?) The third mode of consciousness is that of 'reflection' in which the individual attempts to focus attention on the very operations of consciousness. He is introspective, but he ought to realize that the endeavour is vain. There is no object called the consciousness that he can inspect. To turn the gaze inwards is to turn the gaze on to nothing; therefore there is a tendency to invent an entity called one's consciousness and proceed to contemplate this fiction. Just as one can accept the

85

labels proposed by other people, thus turning oneself into a thing, so one can pretend to solidify one's own consciousness.

In contrast to these false (though normal) forms of consciousness, there is the legitimate type of mental activity, which is extraordinarily difficult to maintain. This consists of a continual awareness of oneself doing things. There is only ceaseless activity. The individual thinks or does something, and is simultaneously aware of the thinking or the doing. Thus he has little tendency to identify himself with objects in the world or with ideas in his own mind. He is alert to the smallest temptation to confuse himself with whatever he is contemplating. He is unremittingly conscious of himself as a void striving to fill itself in some specific way, as a lack trying to become whatever at any particular moment it feels itself to be a lack of. For instance, he is performing the action of rowing and knows that he is to be defined as one who, for some unknown reason, out of all his lacks, has selected his lack of status as complete rower to remedy. His nature lies in this choice, and he avoids bad faith to the extent that he recognizes that it is a free choice and that his aspiration is not fulfilled.

It is necessary now to compare Sartre's notions of consciousness with the earlier notions that I have discussed. Freud's first division of the psyche into consciousness and the unconscious, and his second division into ego, superego and id are both swept aside by Sartre. Perhaps it would be more helpful to say that the Freudian boundaries are removed so that we are left with one encompassing consciousness. To Freud in his later period the ego was a piece of the unconscious that had been split away from the rest, and the superego was a moral attitude absorbed from the parents. Sartre's refutation of Freud is to the effect that the mental processes thus categorized by Freud are all observable. It is true, though, that Sartre pays little or no attention to biological factors, upon which Freud's psychology is firmly based. In Freud there is what must be the correct assumption that the mind, whatever it is, is an attribute of the body, of the brain and nervous system. The original unconscious is the physical basis from which mental consciousness develops. Sartre simply leaves such considerations aside and concentrates exclusively on the structure of consciousness, seen, in the humanistic way, as the only valuable aspect of man.

If we next compare Sartre with Bergson, we can see at once that the older philosopher's twofold division of the individual into a social self and a fundamental self bears some resemblance to Sartre's depiction of three regular forms of consciousness. In particular, being-for-others is one important aspect of the Bergsonian social self, though the latter concept embraces all one's practical transactions with the external world. But a noteworthy difference between the two philosophers lies in the degree of thrusting activity attributed to the mind. In Bergson the social self is the active intermediary between the passive fundamental self and the outside world. It is as if the real self is a passive absorbent of an endless stream of impressions while the social self is a kind of hypocritical go-between who simplifies and distorts these impressions in the interests of survival. Something similar is found in Virginia Woolf and Proust. In Proust the real self comes into being when one perfectly apprehends one's impressions, and Virginia Woolf habitually speaks of people as impinged upon by their impressions. A mind is like a target with arrows raining in upon it from all sides. In these two writers positive activity seems to consist in choosing which impressions to receive: the individual is defined by his personal selection.

In contrast to this, the heroes of Sartre's novels have furiously active intellects. There is an ascending scale of conceptualization from Virginia Woolf to Proust to Sartre. Virginia Woolf's main characters perceive a great deal and reflect but little; Proust's Marcel is both highly perceptive and sinuously reflective, while Sartre's Roquentin (in *Nausea*) and his Mathieu (in *Roads to Freedom*) incessantly seek to explain their perceptions by ideas. In this special sense Sartre's fictions, as compared with Proust's and Virginia Woolf's, celebrate action and choice. His heroes apprehend the world around them as trivial, disgusting or flat, and it is these qualities that must be explained by intellectual action or obliterated by physical action. The climax in a Sartre fiction is typically a moment of choice arrived at spontaneously after a long period of reflection.[8] Thus Roquentin has been seeing the world as weary, stale, flat and unprofitable, and in particular has learned, as he supposes, that the basic stuff of existence is viscous, gluey in composition. In the celebrated and much-analysed episode of Roquentin's looking at the root of a chestnut tree in the public park he realizes that while the root exists as a thing in its own right, independent of his consciousness, it is fundamentally part of a general gluey mess that comprises the entire park and the whole universe of things. The hero's problem is how to escape from this frightful vision which, though it is presumably pathological, is regarded by Sartre as more objectively accurate than the normal way of viewing objects. Roquentin believes that the only avenue of escape is through man-made abstractions, such as mathematics and music. A circle, for example, or a symphony, does not exist, and therefore is not part of the general viscosity. The climax comes when in the cafe Roquentin listens once again to his favourite record, 'Some of these Days', and concludes that the composer of the song and the negress singing it have risen above mere existence by their production of a formally perfect, self-justifying work of art. Roquentin decides that he will save himself from mere existence in the same way, by creating a work of art, probably a novel.

The conclusion of the story of Mathieu (which comes in *Iron in the Soul*, the third volume of *Roads to Freedom*) is similar, to the extent that Mathieu finds release from his usual questioning by joining a number of resistance fighters on a church tower, where they will all certainly be killed. This suicidal action may not be the only logical answer to the sort of problems with which Mathieu has been torturing himself, but it is clearly intended by Sartre to be the right answer in the circumstances. At long last Mathieu has un-equivocally and irrevocably done something.

It is not my purpose to add to the number of analyses of Sartre's novels and stories, but to point to a feature of modern fiction that they exemplify. This of course is the concentration on action and choice, seen existentialistically in terms of self-definition. I make myself and give meaning to the world, not as in Virginia Woolf and Proust by the perfect grasp of my perceptions, but by decision. This is not a rational decision, the end-product of a chain of reasoning; nor is it the consequence of an unconscious impulse in the old sense. In effect the hero suddenly decides that he will discover himself in action rather than by thought. The burden of consciousness, which I discussed in the first chapter, is simply allowed to fall away. The hero has wished to discern his 'true self', on the model of a pre-Einsteinian scientist lighting on the chemical or physical properties of a piece of the natural world: the properties exist independently of the scientist, whose task it is to uncover them. Now the hero realizes that he has no transcendental ego with which to observe and direct his mental states, but is instead whatever he, by his voluntary actions, causes himself to be. The notion can be ex-pressed as a question: How can I know what I am until I see what I do?

Heroes, choices and actions of this type had come into the novel before *Nausea* and before Sartre's theoretical disquisition in *Being and Nothingness*. This is part of what Iris Murdoch means when in her study of Sartre she observes that 'he has the style of the age'. She writes: 'Connexions which elsewhere are subterranean stand clearly traced out in the prolific lucidity of Sartre's work.'[9] Of course Sartre did not invent the existentialist hero, and, indeed, writers on this subject usually begin their surveys with the 1840s, with Kierkegaard and the early Dostoevsky. The fact remains that until about the 1940s most fictional characters were not portrayed in the existen-tialist manner, but from that time onwards a large proportion have been so portrayed.

Nausea came out in 1938, and in the same year Sartre remarked, with special reference to the novel, *U.S.A.*, that 'Dos Passos is the greatest novelist of our time'. I am not concerned to discuss either Dos Passos or this estimate of him but only to mention that Sartre felt that American novelists were expressing a truer vision of life than Frenchmen had recently expressed, including (or especially) Proust.

Sartre's enthusiasm for the American novel is of particular interest. For many years before *Nausea* appeared Hemingway, outstandingly, had been expressing a vision of life that was at once stoical and existentialistic. In Hemingway's books a man is certainly nothing but what he makes of himself in his struggles amid or against an environment that is often beautiful and sometimes destructive. This is an aspect of what critics used to mean when they complained that Hemingway's characters were ill-drawn. Jake Barnes, they said, was' nothing but an impotent expatriate journalist; Fredric Henry was merely an idealistic ambulance-driver in love. Is it not curious, however, that everyone remembers Hemingway's characters very clearly? What we remember is not, as in traditional portraits, a set of idiosyncracies, but the quality of an experience. The experience almost entirely coincides with the character. Lieutenant Henry is nothing more or less than his love affair with Catherine Barkley, the events of the war and the escape. We apprehend him through his feelings and sensations, which are themselves totally linked to the environment. Hemingway portrays an individual by describing what he perceives, and sometimes by giving to him a set of desires or an overriding will.

No doubt it is clear by now that all Hemingway's heroes from Nick Adams to Santiago simply do not exhibit the same mode of being as that which distinguishes the characters of traditional fiction. Nick in 'Indian Camp' is a boy experiencing the sights and sounds of the early morning, watching his father perform the operation, looking at the dead Indian with his cut throat. To have conferred upon Nick any sort of fixed character would have been not only superfluous but also false. This is not just because Nick is an unformed boy in an exceptional situation but chiefly because Hemingway was already, in 1924, seeing individuals in the modern way, as lacking a crystallized personality. It is the same with the old man, Santiago, who is largely comprised of his project, his sensations and, occasionally, his memories. His consciousness is almost exclusively of the sea, the fish, his hero, Dimaggio, and his boy-companion whom he has left behind—all held together by his will to conquer the fish.

Plainly, though, there is a considerable difference between one Hemingway hero and another. Down the years hostile critics have been too busy noting the similarities—that they are men of action,

sensuous rather than intellectual; that they are 'undefeated losers'—
to observe closely enough the differences. Colonel Cantwell, for
instance, has very little in common with Harry Morgan, who in
turn bears almost no resemblance to Robert Jordan. But they differ
as their life-experience differs, and, most importantly, in their
specific objectives. They do not differ by virtue of some indwelling
quality.

This means that when one sets out to define Hemingway's heroes
one describes what they think, feel and do. Neither before their
actions, as a cause of the actions, nor afterwards as a consequence
are they 'characters'. At the end of *To Have and Have Not* Harry
Morgan's wife, after her husband's death, thinks of her situation as
follows: 'Nobody's going to tell me that and there ain't nothing now
but take it every day the way it comes and just get started doing
something right away.' Presumably this conclusion is both the
dourness of an uneducated woman who cannot see any source of
hope for herself, and the author's expression through that woman of
an existentialistic outlook—'just get started doing something right
away'. However, the point is that Marie Morgan is almost entirely
summed up in such words as these, as her husband has been summed
up in his moment-by-moment consciousness of the smuggling trips
between Florida and Cuba. Similarly, Robert Jordan at the end of
For Whom the Bell Tolls concludes that 'there's no *one* thing that's
true'. The whole business with the guerrilla band has been 'true',
just as Jordan's earlier career in Montana once carried its own local
meaning. Jordan has tried to relate his former job as a university
teacher of Spanish to his present task of blowing up the bridge, but
has been unable to see any clear connection. Jordan's disjointed
life may be taken as a gloss on T. S. Eliot's words in 'Ash Wednes-
day': 'And what is actual is actual for only one time/And only for
one place'. It follows that Jordan also has differed in important
respects from one stage in his life to the next. Once when he was a
child his grandfather, who fought in the Civil War, showed him a
pistol; lately he has been the lover of Maria; now he is lying alone
with a broken thigh bone: these phases of consciousness can be
connected principally by the various, scarcely explicable decisions
that Jordan has made.

If an existentialistic view of man can be discerned in some pre-war
American novelists (in Hemingway the view is more clear-cut, I
think, than in Sartre's own choice of Dos Passos), it is pervasive in
American authors of the next generation. When Mailer wrote *The
Naked and the Dead* (1948) he was not, as he became a little later,
versed in the theories of existentialism, but the novel exhibits
similar assumptions about the being of man. I do not refer to the
bleakness of this novel, the futility of its conclusion, but simply to the

characterization. Mailer presents his characters, mainly the members of one reconnaissance patrol, partly through their present thoughts, words and actions, and partly by his device of 'The Time Machine', which ostensibly shows us how each of them was formed from childhood. However there is no question of having been 'formed' in any deterministic sense: each man reacted to his earlier environment—the slums of Boston or the professional military class or whatever it was—in his own chosen way. This is explicit in the case of Croft, the fascist Texan sergeant. Croft as a child and youth faced his surroundings as a cold and deadly hunter. In the appropriate 'Time Machine' section Mailer puts the matter as follows:

No, but why *is* Croft that way?

Oh, there are answers. He is that way because of the corruption-of-society. He is that way because the devil has claimed him for one of his own. It is because he is a Texan, it is because he has renounced God.

He is that kind of man because the only woman he ever loved cheated on him, or he was born that way, or he was having problems of adjustment.[10]

So Mailer ironically rejects a variety of standard answers, as might be delivered by sophisticated or unsophisticated persons, leaving us with the bare conclusion that Croft is, psychologically speaking, a self-made man.

The philosophical core of *The Naked and the Dead* consists of the arguments between General Cummings and Lieutenant Hearn, the former a fairly clear-sighted fascist and the latter a muddled and vacillating liberal. Mailer's own attitudes to these two men and to the points of view they express are never indicated: the reader can detect neither sympathy for Hearn (who is killed towards the end, as the result of a trick by Sergeant Croft) nor admiration for Cummings. It is clear, however, that Cummings, being possessed of psychological insight and power of concentration, has fashioned his own personality, while Hearn is a mish-mash of the political and cultural influences to which he has been exposed. Cummings has made his choice, whereas Hearn has striven to avoid personal choice.

The antagonism between these two characters in Mailer's first novel is a straightforward illustration of a leading preoccupation in the serious fiction of the last twenty years or so. General Cummings has concluded that since values do not originate outside man, there is nothing in the world to prefer to one's own will. Social life is just a clash of wills and the prize is carried off by the person with the greatest determination and the sharpest intelligence. But Hearn is in search of a value-system that transcends the individual man. He knows full well that his own habitual (though not invariable) tendency to accommodate the wills of others can hardly be the answer, for if we all did that the result would be complete inanity.

It happens that in the year of the publication of *The Naked and the Dead* Sartre gave his answer to the question that Mailer raised through the medium of the Cummings-Hearn debate. In *Existentialism is a Humanism* Sartre argued that while man is free to choose himself, he is not free not to choose. Self-choice, one might say, is a categorical imperative. So far Cummings is right and Hearn wrong. But Sartre also accepts Kant's categorical imperative. 'Act', wrote Kant, 'as if the maxim of your action were to become through your will a general natural law.' Sartre writes:

> When we say that man chooses himself, we do mean that every one of us must choose himself; but by that we also mean that in choosing for himself he chooses for all men. For in effect, of all the actions a man may take in order to create himself as he wills to be, there is not one which is not creative, at the same time, of an image of man such as he believes he ought to be.[11]

It follows that if we apply Sartre's criteria to Mailer's characters we see first that Mailer was right to sense (if indeed he did sense it) a kind of superiority in Cummings, based on this man's relative lack of bad faith. Cummings knew that he had made, and must continue to make, himself. His flaw lies in choosing for himself alone, as if the rest of mankind could be relegated to another category. Hearn, on the other hand, is aware of the need to act on behalf of others, but in the absence of some set of laws cannot decide what to do. Hearn fails to realize that he must heroically make up the laws as he goes along.

The political novels of the 1940s pursue this theme in the harsh though uncomplicated sphere of totalitarianism, while many novels of the fifties and sixties delineate the complexities of choice in ordinary domestic life. Orwell's O'Brien in *Nineteen Eighty-Four* and Rubashov's interrogator in Koestler's *Darkness at Noon* accept and provide a rationale for the power-morality that Cummings adumbrates. These two influential novels, one set forty years ahead, the other set in the immediate past, depict political organizations in which the entire notion of self-choice is an evil or an irrelevancy. In *Nineteen Eighty-Four* people are either Party-members or Proles, the former monitored by the Thought-Police and the latter left free to enjoy their mindless activities. The status quo could be undermined only by fully-fledged individuals, but the identity of each Prole is lost before it is born in the routines of work and sensual pleasure, while the identity of each Party-member is defeated by a set of decreed and false ideas. Winston Smith's feeble and foredoomed rebellion is, as O'Brien ably explains to him, an anachronism, a gesture towards an old vice called individualism. Similarly, in *Darkness at Noon* the conflict is between what may be called the 'lower truth', meaning what actually took place, and the 'higher truth', signifying a version of events that is conducive to the prosperity of the cause. Rubashov is enjoined to confess that he has betrayed the Party on the sophistical grounds that such an 'ideal' betrayal is superior to a merely material loyalty.

Each of these novels is 'existentialistic' only in the elementary sense of attacking social organizations that outlaw personal choice. Every man, says Sartre, must create his own values: no man in *Nineteen Eighty-Four* and *Darkness at Noon* may trust his own perceptions, let alone erect values upon the basis of such perceptions. These novels aim to undermine that extreme form of 'essentialism' whose adherents would superimpose by force and terror the non-existent—Big Brother or Rubashov's treachery—upon the existent. Big Brother, after all, is pure essence, an imaginary figure who is the sum and apex of the characteristics of Oceania. O'Brien, who faithfully serves Big Brother, is more an idealist than a practitioner of *realpolitik*. It might also be said that Newspeak is an ideal language, which expresses not what is true but what the hierarchy think ought to be true; while doublethink is the name of a mental device for promoting purely ideal concepts above concepts that summarize the real world.

In more humdrum circumstances other characters in other novels of the same period were deciding or failing to decide how to make themselves and how to generate their own values. Camus's Meursault is an existentialist in practice rather than in theory, for he is ignorant of the theory. Throughout *The Outsider* he behaves in accordance with his own perceptions and inclinations. In his drifting way (partly vacuous but often acute) he seems to know that a value cannot simply be received—from society, from tradition, from the Church—but until the end he fails to understand why his knowledge makes him an object of vilification to many other people. His spontaneous rejection of the priest's belief in an after-life makes him realize why he is hated and that he has been right to pursue his own course. He has unthinkingly refused to participate in a game—a worldly game, for all its spiritual pretensions. He seems finally to understand that it is precisely because there is, so far as we can possibly know, no life after death that life before death must be lived with complete honesty. Implicit in this story is the notion asserted plainly in *The Myth of Sisyphus* of making rather than receiving value and identity. Meursault is inchoate: his character, until just before his execution, consists in a lack of character. He is a fitful will and a consciousness recording events and personalities with some discrimination but little purpose, a living fragment of the hot Algerian coast. It is his distinction that he is incapable of accepting a ready-made identity or of attributing to himself a soul.

Meursault is not a tragic hero, though his ending is, in a manner, heroic and of course many existentialist heroes are conspicuously unheroic figures cast in the mould of comedy. Often enough they are stuck in the first stage of existentialist progress, the stage of rejection. This is so, for instance, in the case of Salinger's Holden Caulfield in *The Catcher in the Rye*. What Holden perceives from first to last is that everyone except himself is engaged in some elaborate game or other. He encounters the game of school, the game of psycho-analysis, the game of writing for films (which his brother has taken up with disgusting success) the family game, and so on. The phoney-ness with which Holden is surrounded and about which he makes his endless comical complaint consists only of the ordinary manoeuv-res of social intercourse: people pose, strike attitudes, 'play at' being schoolmasters or doctors or mothers. It would be wrong to suppose that in this novel Salinger was attacking rich Easterners or champion-ing the young against the middle-aged, for such factors are incidental. *The Catcher in the Rye* illustrates what Eric Berne later discussed in his work of popular psychology, *Games People Play* (1964), which amounts to a lively exposition of some common forms of bad faith.

At best Holden Caulfield is an existentialist hero in embryo. He refuses to indulge in what Heidegger called 'forgetfulness of existence' (heedlessness of the quality of what one is doing, bearing firmly in mind the fact of death), but is not mature or confident enough to do more than squirm before the ubiquitous insincerities.

By the time of *Franny and Zooey* (1961) Salinger had progressed from this phase of rejection to a phase of affirmation. Throughout this later novel Franny Glass, the youngest child of the brilliant, unstable Irish-Jewish Glass family, is in a position not unlike Holden Caulfield's in the earlier novel: she is bewildered, frightened, on the verge of a breakdown. Her brother Zooey (Zachary) is somewhat ahead of her in the search for values, though both these children have been the recipients of careful religious instruction from two elder brothers, Seymour and Buddy. Seymour, it seems, was the pioneer in pursuit of a satisfactory way of life. He came to be an adherent of Zen Buddhism and before his suicide collaborated with Buddy in preparing a body of advice to pass on to the two youngest members of the family. This advice Buddy retails to Franny in a letter, but she cannot accept it. Only at the end of the novel, in a long telephone conversation, does Zooey impart to Franny the meaning that Salinger himself intends. This may be baldly summarized as following the way of life that suits one (loving one's fate) and regarding as sacred every individual human being, however vulgar or stupid. In particular terms, Franny must 'shoot for some kind of perfection' as an actress and love the 'Fat Lady', who is every single person in the audience, of whatever degree of freakishness and ignobility.

The important point here is not Salinger's own love-ethic, which has often been found mawkish and banal, but the mere fact that Salinger did pursue through Holden Caulfield and the various tales of the Glass family, culminating in *Franny and Zooey*, an exploration that can reasonably be described as existentialistic.

An exploration of this kind has become almost the norm in serious American fiction of the last twenty years or so. Sometimes the novel presents us with the mere breakdown of traditional values and traditional assumptions about the nature of being. John Updike's *Rabbit, Run*, for example, is the portrait of a man, Harry Angstrom, who is, or could be, a great success in all manner of accepted ways: sport, business, sex. What he desires, however, is some kind of achievement that confers meaning on the entire world. It seems that it is unsatisfactory to be only a basketball star, for instance, because (and this in direct contradiction to Salinger's view at the end of *Franny and Zooey*) such an achievement represents a local kind of perfection. As a man in pursuit of utter perfection, Angstrom is of saintly disposition: he 'runs' from one activity to another looking for whatever is without blemish or limitedness.

Perhaps, however, it is Saul Bellow, who, among American novelists of the post-war period, has most consistently and on a large scale tackled his variegated subject-matter in the existentialist spirit. In Bellow's first novel, *Dangling Man* (1944) the hero-narrator, Joseph, writes in his journal as follows:

> The quest, I am beginning to think, whether it be for money, for notoriety, reputation, increase of pride, whether it leads us to thieving, slaughter, sacrifice, the quest is one and the same. All the striving is for one end. I do not entirely understand this impulse. But it seems to me that its final end is the desire for pure freedom.[12]

These words were written before Bellow could have formed much familiarity with Sartre's theories (though he might have been influenced by the diary-form and some of the ideas of *Nausea*) and possibly before he had read earlier existentialist philosophers, such as Heidegger and Jaspers, but the tentative conclusion ascribed to the character, Joseph, resembles Sartre's positive assertions in *Being and Nothingness*. Man's questing activities, writes Joseph, are undertaken out of a desire for pure freedom: 'human reality', writes

Sartre—much more sweepingly—'is a perpetual surpassing towards a coincidence with itself which is never given.'[13] Only God coincides perfectly with Himself, is without shortcoming or limitation, is purely free. Sartre states:

> For freedom is nothing other than a choice which creates for itself its own possibilities, but it appears here that the initial project of being God, which 'defines' man, comes close to being the same as a human 'nature' or 'essence'.[14]

In other words, man is, as Bellow's early protagonist surmised, a creature who aims to be God, 'pure freedom', and does so without knowing it through his chosen activities, which may be thievery or sacrifice. Bellow's later protagonists continue the quest inaugurated by Joseph. Asa Leventhal in *The Victim* is engaged throughout his story in a species of combat with a certain Kirby Allbee, a depressive anti-semite whose theme is that a good deal of human suffering is gratuitous. This may seem a truism, but Allbee argues that Leventhal, a comfortably-off Jew, has unthinkingly accepted the 'Jewish' belief that pain is somehow merited, 'right', ordained by God. Allbee illustrates this argument by reference to Jewish history and culture, notably the Book of Job.

Once again in this novel Bellow is concerned with the nature and limits of freedom, and consequently he sets up a protagonist who tends to assume that life is more or less manageable and an antagonist who wallows in despair. The author's implicit and tentative conclusion—which is reached after Allbee has tried to arrange a suicide for both himself and Leventhal—is to the effect that mankind has limitless responsibilities but limited capacities. In relation to the main characters of the novel this means that Leventhal has been wrong to disregard the bulk of human misery, on the unexamined but not necessarily incorrect grounds that people frequently deserve what they get, while Allbee has been too prone to treat suffering as an outrage.

Asa Leventhal has his final existentialistic stance forced upon him, and this is true also of Tommy Wilhelm in *Seize the Day*, who arrives at an understanding of himself after a day of humiliations even more acute than the humiliations he has regularly suffered in the past. The point about a Bellow hero is that he has to discover his own values in an environment that offers conflicting and unsatisfactory models. He may be impelled towards such a discovery, as are Leventhal and Wilhelm, or he may actively pursue it, as do Augie March and Moses Herzog. The 'environment' varies intellectually as well as geographically and means the entire world the hero encounters 'in his head' as well as physically. Thus Joseph's environment is little more than his city circumstances as a clerk waiting to be drafted into the army, while Augie March's environments include the Chicago slums, Mexico and Europe; but the environments of such later heroes as Herzog and Sammler embrace old Europe, tracts of assimilated history and vast reading in philosophy. Herzog and Sammler, in the midst of their exasperating personal relationships and in the face of the vivid harshnesses of New York City (Herzog in the courtroom, for instance; Sammler in his encounter with the negro pickpocket) attempt to find a path, a meaning for themselves that excludes nothing of which they are conscious. Herzog must find a meaning that subsumes his actual relations with his estranged wife, Madeleine, his awareness of the sights, sounds and smells of the city, his forefathers' tales of Russia, and his own knowledge of, say, Kierkegaard or Spinoza or Emerson. Sammler, who is also a formidable intellectual, has a similar range of information to process, as one might say, in order to arrive at a solution.

Thus Bellow takes into account both the phenomenal world, so throughly faced by the older American writers, such as Hemingway and Dos Passos, and the intellectualized world of such European writers as Sartre. There is an attempted fusion of ideas and sensuous experiences, combined with the portraits of keen emotional entanglements.

I have discussed Bellow at some length because in his works the existentialist concept of being, of individuals discerning or attempting to discern their own meanings in whatever portions of the world they encounter, is so conspicuous. But other leading novelists of our time (especially in America) exhibit the same tendency, though less obtrusively. Even, for example, such vividly dissimilar writers as William Styron and Carson McCullers have this much in common. Though they are so different in style and vision, each portrays a world that lacks a given meaning. Traditional values, at least in their readily accessible forms, are absent from the conclusions of both Styron's *Lie Down in Darkness* and such a story as Carson McCullers's 'Reflections in a Golden Eye'. There is only the representation of confusion, perhaps merely and intentionally jarring in the Styron novel; certainly aesthetically pleasing in Carson McCullers's story.

One could multiply examples, but at this stage it will be more profitable to turn to a consideration of existential psychology: afterwards it will be possible to reach some conclusions about the relationship of that branch of psychology to the contemporary novel.

6

A NEW SYNTHESIS

Existential Psychology and the Contemporary Novel

We have been examining a recent phase of a development the beginnings of which lie in the seventeenth century with Newton, Descartes and the rise of science. This development consists of man's sense of displacement from his firm position in the natural scheme and of various attempts to reintegrate man with nature. In the immediate post-Darwin period there was a fresh emphasis on a gulf between human consciousness and the rest of the world. Part of the reason for this was, as we have seen, the supposition that the 'lower' instincts were directly opposed to the 'higher' elements of consciousness, an old attitude given peculiar force by the lessening of belief in the Christian God. For now man's best characteristics seemed to some thinkers to be defenceless, without support or authority. I have presented Freud's argument that the lower instincts are the roots from which higher aspirations grow as an attempt to reconcile man and nature. According to this view man is not an essentially rational being bedevilled by instincts; on the contrary he is a creature whose power of reason owes its very vitality to the energy of the instincts. He is like a plant thrusting upwards through the soil, and sometimes bearing glorious fruits, but never capable of subsisting without its roots. In this way reason, the highest faculty, is irrevocably linked with nature through the medium of natural, instinctual energies.

Still, Freud's case depended on assigning the instincts to the un-conscious, so that there remained a barrier in the psyche on one side of which was the ego, the real 'I' (or the place where the 'I' was located), while the id remained on the other side. The ego was the subject, and the id, like any component of the world of nature, was the object. Freud's assumption was that the subject-ego would gradually acquire greater knowledge of the object-id, and so become more free.

Philosophers might well see Freud's central thesis as a chapter in the history of dualism, a doctrine that began with Plato and was more or less rounded off by Descartes.[1] But though Descartes nearly completed what Plato began, the doctrine has a later history that largely consists of the attempts of thinkers (including non-philosophers, such as Freud) to refute it. Descartes believed that the body acts on the mind and the mind on the body, but that the two are distinct from each other, and this is the general assumption to the present day. The body is part of the great universe of matter; it obeys the laws of physics and chemistry; it is positioned in space and time. The mind, however, is of a different order of being. We still find it almost impossible to think in other terms than these.

Freud was an enthusiast for science in the late nineteenth-century manner. He regarded the psyche as a collection of neurobiological activities which, since we experience them as thoughts, feelings, etc., could be studied from a psychological point of view. They could and should also be studied from the biological standpoint, so that eventually biologists and psychologists working from different ends would 'meet in the middle', and the mind-body problem would be solved.

Freud therefore was not a dualist: in his explicit view mind was totally dependent on matter. The tenor of Freud's work is such that we can assume that he would have agreed with the following remarks of T. H. Huxley:

> We are conscious automata, endowed with free will in the only intelligible sense of that much-abused term—in as much as in many respects we are able to do as we like—but nonetheless parts of the great series of causes and effects which, in unbroken continuity, composes that which is, and has been, and shall be— the sum of existence.[2]

Thus T. H. Huxley placed man firmly in the natural scheme without denying him a fair amount of free will, and Freud's writings indicate a similar conception. But some novelists and psychologists coming after Freud (that is, after the first impact of Freud's ideas) felt a need to bridge the dualistic gap firmly and completely now, not in the future when the workings of the mind-body have become more fully understood. What was desiderated was the unification of subject and object, of perceiver and perceived, which should come about without either falsification of the object or annihilation of the subject. Proust and Virginia Woolf, in their nevertheless rather different ways, saw the solution in terms of absolute fidelity to one's impressions: paradoxically the individual is most united with the external world when he is most himself. Put the other way round, the surest way to increase the gulf between one's consciousness and everything else (to grow alienated and, in the end, mad) is to identify oneself with the external world in the wrong way. This wrong way consists of trying to superimpose impressions apparently received by others upon the impressions naturally received by oneself. The more one is aware of the otherness of the Other, the more one will feel a healthy affinity with him. Many post-Freudian psychologists have come to the same conclusion.

Nevertheless in psychological and philosophical theory, if not always in day-to-day experience, there has remained a dichotomy between man as subject and the world as his object, a rift that many thinkers and creative writers have in recent times sought to heal. Increasingly from about the time of the Second World War there has developed a desire for cultural forms that will immerse man in the world, thus diminishing his role as observer, experimental scientist or critic. In various aspects of popular culture and in some modish highbrow theories this desire has resulted in a derogation of intellect, enthusiasm for mindless group activities, neo-primitivism, a hostility to reason, to discrimination, and to discipline. But such contemporary attitudes exemplify the usual debasement of subtle and promising ideas. The attempts of some philosophers and psychologists to involve man thoroughly in his world are quite different from the fashionable antics that are their vulgar counter-part. Among the philosophers there is a shift from the notion of a contemplative self to the notion of an active self: we act upon the world rather than observing it, and whatever observations we do make are in the service of actions. Among the psychologists there is an increasing sense that the individual is an integrated organism responding to particular, present situations. This entails the abolition of the old faculty-psychology (cognition, conation, etc., are now seen as artificial divisions) and even a blurring of the distinction between the mind and the body. It entails also a neglect of, or an outright assault upon, the notion of the unconscious. It is maintained that there is no actual division in the psyche; no psychic entity housed in the body, and, in a state of health, no *experienced* (as opposed to theoretical) separation between an individual and the particular piece of the world of which at any particular moment he happens to be a part. In this chapter I shall mention some of these latter-day philosophical and psychological views and then discuss their implications for notions of value and character in the novel.

It is best to begin with an excursion into recent metaphysics, because in metaphysical writings we shall find openly and cogently discussed some notions that are implicit in works of psychology and in novels. Gilbert Ryle's *The Concept of Mind* has probably been the most celebrated British contribution to contemporary metaphysical discussion, and, curiously enough, for all its conspicuous Britishness, it is reminiscent here and there of Sartre's ideas.

Ryle's manner is almost the opposite of Sartre's. He is carefully and wittily logical, using a multitude of homely illustrations but few metaphors and no dramatic set-pieces. He accounts for mental operations rather than describing or dramatizing them. He begins by asserting that the usual concept of mind, which stems chiefly from Descartes, is false: he calls it 'the dogma of the Ghost in the Machine'. He says that we have here a category-mistake. It is as if a foreigner visiting Oxford or Cambridge for the first time were shown the various colleges, administrative offices, etc., and then enquired of his guide, 'But where is the University?' Similarly we are aware of such activities as thinking, feeling and imagining, but we go on to assume that the notion, 'mind', belongs to the same category as these activities. In fact 'mind' is merely a designation of aspects of our behaviour.

Ryle proceeds to examine knowledge (of the world and of the self), the will, emotion, sensation, imagination, and the intellect. These concepts are discussed in behavioural, though not behaviouristic, terms. Language disposes us to think of the 'will', for example, as if it were an actual, indwelling thing, but really there is only the process of desiring or working towards some end. Furthermore, so-called 'inner' forms of behaviour are not essentially different from 'outer' forms. If I will something without expressing my will in any way, then I have simply failed to express it. Similarly, silent thoughts are thoughts that are not uttered. Ryle claims that keeping one's thoughts to oneself is a positive accomplishment that follows learning how to speak. The infant is not a mass of unexpressed thoughts who later acquires speech: on the contrary, he learns to think by learning to speak, and after that he learns how to talk and think 'in his head'. Ryle writes:

> People tend to identify their minds with the 'place' where they conduct their secret thoughts. They even come to suppose that there is a special mystery about how we publish our thoughts instead of realising that we employ a special artifice to keep them to ourselves.[3]

In such ways as I am briefly indicating, Ryle attempts not so much to modify as to destroy the concept of mind, replacing it by descriptions of typical behaviour. Along with Sartre, though employing quite different arguments, he maintains that there is no central 'I', no transcendental ego. There are only acts and 'higher order' acts. A higher order act is an act which is performed upon another act. Thus, if I bowl a cricket ball and simultaneously or in retrospect think about myself bowling the ball, then the thinking is a higher order act. (It is not necessarily a superior kind of act.) Because we are able to do this sort of thing, we come to believe that there is a special 'I' governing or at least observing our behaviour. This special 'I' has always eluded philosophical enquiry because it doesn't exist: there is only the usual 'I', the subject, who observes himself in the same way that he observes others.

In the final chapter of *The Concept of Mind*, as a culmination of urbane and systematic demolitions of common notions about mental processes, Ryle says in effect that there can be no such study as psychology in one of its common meanings. There can be no study of the mind as such, though there can be systematic investigations of behaviour; there can be psycho-therapy, and there can be attempts to elucidate strange patterns of behaviour. Mechanistic and materialistic though this type of advocacy may sound to some readers, it is matched by the practice of most contemporary novelists and by the arguments of many contemporary psychologists who are opposed to the materialistic schools. However, before we return to the novel and to psychology proper there is another philosopher whose contentions we should briefly consider.

John MacMurray's influential book, *The Self as Agent*, is another attempt to overthrow the notion of the self as aloofly contemplative. Just as Gilbert Ryle disbelieves in the existence of an entity called 'the mind' and argues that there is no separate 'I', so, from quite another point of view, Professor MacMurray contends that the self is merely the whole person acting upon the world. After initial assertions that the 'form of the personal is the emergent problem of contemporary philosophy'[4] and a chapter dealing with the relationship between Kant's Critical philosophy and romanticism, MacMurray goes on to argue that action and thought are not separable from each other, as we have usually been led to believe, and are certainly not opposed to each other. Acting and thinking are not 'exclusive contraries' but the 'ideal limits of personal experience'. Pure thought never takes place, for it would be completely formal, without content, which is an impossibility. On the other hand action is invariably accompanied by some sort of thinking.

The self, MacMurray maintains, is always in some form of cause-and-effect relationship with the world: it is not a distinct subject examining the world, but an agent acting upon the world.

Consider now the Self in relation to the world. When I act I modify the world. Action is causally effective, even if it fails of the particular effect that is intended. This implies that the Self is part of the world in which it acts, and in dynamic relation with the rest of the world. On the other hand, as subject the Self stands 'ever against' the world, which is its object. The Self as subject then is not part of the world it knows, but withdrawn from it, and so, in conception, outside it, or other than its object. But to be part of the world is to exist, while to be excluded from the world is to be non-existent. It follows that the Self exists as agent but not as subject.[5]

This extract has the air of a key passage in *The Self as Agent*, yet out of context it is unconvincing. The Self is obviously a subject, whether it is contemplating or acting upon a piece of the world. MacMurray presumably intends to annihilate not the distinction between subject and object but the notion that they are, or could be, disconnected. He is saying that there is no Self that first exists and then performs some action or other: apart from its actions it is non-existent, a philosophical abstraction. And thought is also a mode of action, he considers, in that it is designed to have some effect on the world. Therefore the Self is an agent, wholly and inescapably connected with the world.

But what is the self? Is it something housed in the body, analagous to old, naive notions of the soul or to pre-Rylean concepts of mind? MacMurray contends that the body–mind problem is 'fictitious'. 'When I act, therefore, my consciousness—my seeing, hearing, remembering, thinking—does not *accompany* but is *integrated* with my bodily movements and is a part-determinant of them.'[6] So the self is simply the whole individual, thoughts as well as physical movements (distinctions between which are largely if not entirely artificial) and the self's relations with other objects and persons are active and modificatory rather than contemplative.

Furthermore this self, this agent-self, is free and not determined. The past alone is determined (what's done can't be undone), while the future is always open. If it were not open it would not be the future. Action in the present is what creates the future. But it is the sole function of the self to act: therefore the self makes actual what was merely possible, or, in other words, freely brings about the future.

It will be clear from these brief references to the theme of *The Self as Agent*, coupled with the better-known arguments of *The Concept of Mind*, that recent British metaphysics has affinities with the continental, especially the Sartrean, variety. Of course there are great differences as well, but we need to concern ourselves with only one important fact: that there is an emergent view of the human individual as whole, purposeful, and self-determining within the limits of natural law. He is whole because his mind is neither set apart from his body nor divisible into categories; he is purposeful in the sense that his nature forces him to actualize possibilities, and he is self-determining because his choice of projects constitutes his character. These remarks, which correlate the views of Sartre, Ryle and MacMurray, are not intended to minimize the constraints (of physique, environment, and heredity) upon any individual; nor should they be taken as support for the infantile, Promethean dream of freedom, in which actions do not have their appropriate consequences.

It is not surprising that parallel views are held by some latter-day psychologists. To be accurate, the attitudes of modern existentialist psychologists are derived from writings produced in the earlier decades of the century, so that what we are considering is a development that overlapped to some extent with the growth of psychoanalysis.

In 1913, the year in which Jung published his *Psychology of the Unconscious* and three years before Freud began delivering his *Introductory Lectures on Psycho-Analysis*, there appeared the original German edition of Karl Jaspers's *General Psychopathology*. Jaspers, then a psychiatrist, argued that human existence was fundamentally 'a form of inward behaviour, a grasp of self, a self-election, a self-appropriation',[7] and therefore could not be studied as a scientist studies natural objects. Recent existentialist psychologists would not necessarily express the matter in the same way, but they all disapprove of the objectification of human beings. Human life is held to be radically different from other forms of life, not of course on the grounds that people have souls, nor even because man has a larger brain and a greater consciousness than other creatures, but for reasons that can best be explained—and often are explained—by reference to Heidegger's notion of *Dasein*.

Dasein, a key term in Heidegger's *Being and Time* (originally *Sein und Zeit*, 1927), means literally 'being there'. Heidegger uses the word to denote the quality of being of human being: a person in his or her fundamental nature is always there, in the world. In other words an individual does not possess a distinct nature that meets or interacts with each of his myriad environments, but rather his nature wholly consists of his encounters with his environments. Furthermore, the being of human being is essentially illuminative of the world. This means that a depopulated world would be a meaningless world. It is not that such a world would lack inherent properties, but that its properties acquire meaning only in the presence of a suitably endowed creature to whom they can disclose themselves. In this sense disclosure and meaning are one and the same. However in all probability man is the only creature who can thus receive the meaning of things, and the ability—or rather the need—to do so is more than an attribute of man: it is his very nature.

104

Fifty years after Heidegger's first formulations of these ideas they are still hard to accept because they are alien to Western tradition, and perversions of the ideas in the direction of subjective idealism are all around us. But we are now concerned with existential psychology whose exponents for the most part do not thus distort Heidegger's central theme. Of the well-known existentialist psychologists it is Medard Boss, on his own account, who adheres most completely to Heidegger's philosophy, while others preach various forms of 'revisionism', but all argue with a Heideggerean frame of reference. Boss, a Swiss psychiatrist, calls his system 'Daseins-analysis', while the approach of Ludwig Binswanger, another Swiss, is known as 'Existential Analysis'. Rollo May is the best-known American in this field and R. D. Laing the best-known Briton.

Medard Boss's book, *Psychoanalysis and Daseinsanalysis* is largely a comparison between Freud's ideas and his own, to the advantage of the latter. Boss states that Freud's system is an examination of the so-called psyche with certain norms in mind. Thus hallucination is regarded by Freud as a derangement of the psyche, a flooding into the consciousness of unconscious material. But in Daseinsanalysis everything is seen in terms of the individual's immediate life-situation, his *Dasein*, his relationship with the world. A hallucination has a certain validity, for it is a revelation to the individual of his actual relationship with other persons. (As a matter of fact Jung frequently wrote in this way, as if bizarre mental phenomena should be treated respectfully on their own terms, but he of course was absolutely wedded to the notion of the unconscious, which Boss rejects.)

The Daseinsanalytic method—in ordinary life as well as in therapy—is to respond fully to one's situations, rather as a healthy child does, with a minimum of preconceptions. Boss writes:

In sharp contradistinction to this natural–scientific approach to man's nature, the approach of Freud, in particular, the Daseins-analytic science of man and his world asks us for once just to look at the phenomena of our world themselves, as they confront us, and to linger with them sufficiently long to become fully aware of what they tell us directly about their meaning and essence.[8]

Things are what they seem; there is nothing 'behind' the appearance. To say this is not to dismiss conjuring tricks, deceptions, misjudgments and optical illusions. The swindler says one thing and means another, but his plausible smile is itself a reality. So is the apparent bend in a stick under water. Appearance and reality are the same in the sense that, for example, sexual desire is not the felt operation of an underlying sexual instinct: the so-called 'instinct' is the desire and, apart from physical manifestations, it is nothing else.

Just as Gilbert Ryle sought to destroy the usual concept of mind, so Medard Boss implicitly tilts against the usual concept of the 'self'. Of course Boss enjoins people to 'be themselves', as the common phrase has it, but there seems to be no self as such. So deeply ingrained are our idealistic assumptions that when someone is told that he should aim to be himself, he is liable to cast about for his 'self', as one looks for an object. Either he desperately concludes that he lacks identity, or he starts play-acting. Boss repeatedly asserts that an individual is always 'out in the world', meaning that identity and relationships are one and the same. 'To thine own self be true' therefore means: see what you are in fact seeing and not what notions, doctrines or other persons say you are seeing.

Such a view is likely to be thought egotistical or solipsistic, but Boss justly argues that it is not. There is no advocacy of subjectivist imbecilities or of romantic individualism. It is obviously true that what one is 'seeing' may not be there. The expression on the other's face may be benevolent, but one is perhaps paranoic and the expression is interpreted as threatening; leering faces confront the victim of hallucination. Boss's point is, of course, that such phenomena as these occur only to those who have systematically evaded their own true vision of things. We might add—leaving aside severely pathological distortions—that even ordinary mis-interpretations are often due to egotistical interference with the individual's natural view of a situation: the confidence trickster or the plain hypocrite has to play upon his victim's rapacity or self-esteem or some similar obfuscating tendency. A person's rapacity thwarts rather than defines his real nature because it falsifies his perceptions.

It will be seen that this line of thought amounts to yet another assault on old-fashioned (but still widely entertained) beliefs about 'character'. A person has a 'character', which is to say that he is defined by a number of habitual tendencies. The individual is composed of his qualities of character: he has little or no personal nature apart from them, and the patterns of his behaviour manifest them. It is understood, of course, that a person may behave un-characteristically, that his qualities may contradict one another, that he may mould his own character, and that his character might undergo changes, but it is still assumed that his character and his self are more or less the same thing.

On this view to part from one's behaviour-patterns is to part from oneself. More precisely, it may be possible to change, for example, from being habitually melancholy to being habitually sanguine, but it is not possible not to be habitually something or other. This seems to be true, yet it is clear from *Psychoanalysis and Daseinsanalysis* that Boss would regard one's *Dasein*, one's 'being-there', as liable to be hindered by character. The true self is this *Dasein*: it is not the character. The individual is theoretically capable of a multitude of responses because he receives a multitude of impressions. His *raison d'être* is to illuminate the world and, whether he knows it or not, he takes in the meaning of each of his situations. But his character consists of tendencies to ignore some aspects of the meaning and to over-emphasize others, and this perversion of the vision is a perversion of the self.

Of course this existentialistic view of man is open to misunderstandings, the most common of which has recently shown itself in fashionable talk about 'authenticity'. To be 'authentic' often meant to be self-regarding, wilful and asocial. However, the implication of Boss's writings (and of the writings of other serious psychologists) is that a fully-developed individual is primarily and realistically concerned with others. He engages in what the neo-Freudians, as I have mentioned in an earlier chapter, call 'mature object-relations'. This phrase rather amusingly implies that the best way to avoid regarding the other as one's object is to cease viewing him as an extension of oneself, the subject.

It is also the best way to avoid regarding oneself as an object. In schizophrenia, the extreme of 'immature object-relations', the individual has so far come to distrust his own subjective apprehensions as to manufacture what R. D. Laing calls a 'false-self system', through which he attempts or pretends to see the world as he supposes others would have him see it. In other words, the 'split' that the word 'schizophrenia' denotes is a split between the pristine vision and the concocted outer personality. The evidence of one's own senses is not to be trusted because it will be held by others to be a sign that one is an unacceptable, unlovable person. Therefore one erects a 'lovable' false self beneath which cowers a 'detestable' true self.

Laing's first book, *The Divided Self* (1960), is what the author calls 'an existential study in sanity and madness'. It is a description of schizophrenia and of the processes of becoming schizophrenic, but it also embraces commoner and less morbid conditions of a similar type. Because the book is an 'existential study', description of these states and explanation of them amount to the same thing. There is the familiar existentialistic attack on the old categories such as ego, superego, id, etc., and a Heideggerean emphasis on being-in-the world. The schizophrenic has to be understood on his own terms: his crazy remarks express a truth. For instance, a patient says that he is an 'unreal man', which is an eccentric thing to say, but what he means is that he has spent his life acting the part of a 'real man' (making the same responses as other people) and can no longer keep up the pretence. This patient is under the impression that other people possess a solid kind of reality like the reality of objects, while he is a void: consequently he has tried to objectivize himself.

Now, the interesting point here is that in all varieties of existential psychology it is maintained (with Heidegger and Sartre) that every person is indeed a void, pure subjectivity. Boss's idea that a human being is essentially illuminative of the environment means that a human being is not remotely thing-like and is therefore able to receive meaning. Actually he can only receive meaning, and make responses or choices, but cannot himself statically *be* anything. The argument of *The Divided Self* is that the schizophrenic cultivates a thing-like outer self, which includes his body, as a means of guarding what he apprehends as a disembodied and exquisitely vulnerable inner self. It should be added that Laing's later works, especially *Reason and Violence* (1964), move outwards, as it were, from examinations of schizophrenia to socio-political considerations that are thoroughly Sartrean and thoroughly based on a belief that the self is constituted by personal perception, responses and choices that are liable to be 'disconfirmed' by other individuals and by ordinary social conditions.[9]

At this point we can summarize the particular modern concept of man with which we have been dealing. He is a biological product, totally subservient to natural laws but distinguished from other biological products by his capacity to irradiate the universe. Although he must discern meaning and value, he may not manufacture meaning and value purely in accordance with his own wishes and fears; he cannot, furthermore, postulate an invisible reality above or behind appearances, and, except in the natural sciences, he cannot differentiate himself from the field of his care and concern.

So many thinkers have lately been asserting or implying this view of man that it might well be called the modern theme. But the view is not yet commonplace, even among intellectuals, and expressions of it are usually so specialized or partisan, or so entangled in wider political and social considerations that it has been necessary here to develop in reasonably plain language the ontological core of the matter. And of course there is widespread hostility to the view on the grounds that it is irrational and destructive of valuable elements in the western tradition.

It is indeed destructive of western modes of thinking since Plato. Modern though this type of thinking is, writers on existentialism in relation to Western philosophy contend that the new philosophy takes up where the pre-Socratics left off. According to this opinion, expressed most comprehensively by Heidegger, Plato imparted a subject-object dichotomy to Western thought, which led to immense advances but which is now played out. There are two diametrically opposed paths of knowledge: the first, inaugurated by Plato, studies the object and hence gives rise to science, but also ultimately to fear and isolation; the second immerses man in the world. Neither path is superior to the other, but there comes a time when a people must go back to the fork and start down the other path. Clearly for westerners the other path resembles oriental philosophy, but Heidegger believed that it would be futile simply to adopt eastern cultural forms, which are products of different histories, different economic and social conditions. It is not a question of trying, absurdly, to jettison the past, but of thinking again from the beginning with the weight of Western achievement in mind.

On this analysis the burden of consciousness expressed with special urgency by some novelists at the turn of the century (though it was obviously not confined to novelists nor to that brief period), was the product of a dying tradition. The central feature of the phase was, and to a degree still is, an apparent need to grasp through the intellect what is not intellectually comprehensible. Of course it is not maintained that such European and American novelists as those discussed earlier in this book suffered directly from the inadequacy of rational understanding—they were novelists, not philosophers—but that they dramatized the consequent distress. The only impressive symbols they could produce were symbols of disassociation or endurance.

What they felt dissociated from was, quite simply, the object, because a mere connection between consciousness and thing or person seemed no connection at all in the absence of symbols of universal connectedness. Until recently we all grew up believing that things can only be unified from the outside—by God, by the Absolute—but the various thinkers, psychologists and novelists whom I have dealt with in this book were, despite their differences, all engaged in trying to unify things from the inside. Christians assume this cannot be done, whereas non-Christian existentialists assume that it has to be done. So did Jung, Lawrence, Virginia Woolf and Proust, and of course many others whom I have not mentioned. It is easily possible to reproduce remarks by a great variety of modern thinkers that reveal a similar conception of the self or of being; a conception that, if we except such remarkably prophetic figures as Kierkegaard and Dostoevsky, was merely adumbrated here and there in the nineteenth century. Thus D. T. Suzuki, the influential writer on Zen Buddhism, asserts that 'Man is free when he denies himself, and is absorbed in the whole'; that, 'Self is to know itself without going out of itself', and that 'The Self is ever moving or becoming'. The general idea here is that the self

109

is a process rather than a fixed state, pattern or entity, and that it is realized only in its awareness of the rest of the world. It doesn't 'go out of itself' (as in introspection or scientific enquiry) in order to know itself. When Suzuki goes on to contend against 'affective contamination' of the mind or 'the interference of the conscious mind predominated by intellection',[10] we can instantly see his affinity with such men as Lawrence, Proust and Jung. Similarly, the psychologist, Erich Fromm, echoes Lawrence and Jung when he proclaims that 'Birth is not one act: it is a process. The aim of life is to be fully born, though its tragedy is that most of us die before we are thus born.' The unconscious, says Fromm, is merely what one is unaware of in one's reactions. Attitudes are dramas, fictions, and the more one is aware of an attitude, the more one realizes its fictional nature. There is something akin to Lawrence here, and to the existentialists, psychologists or philosophers. Another American psychologist, Abraham Maslow, writes in the same vein when, in various books, he argues that each lifetime should manifest continuous growth of the personality and that the best thinking is invariably 'holistic', a spontaneous, open-minded application of all relevant faculties. Science, including psychology, has been too exclusively rational and too wedded to approved methodologies. Likewise, Anthony Storr, the British (Jungian) psychiatrist, maintains that there is an innate drive towards 'self-realization'. This drive is neither a luxury nor a self-indulgence, but rather has the nature of an instinct. Yet another psychologist, Richard De Martino, expresses this central theme most succinctly, and also most abstractly, as follows:

As an ever object-oriented subject, for the ego to approach this actualization it is usually necessary that every possible content for its object-orientation be spent, depleted or denied.[11]

Out of context these words may be difficult to follow, but what De Martino means is that (as preached in theology, mysticism and many branches of ethics) for self-realization to occur it is necessary for the ego to die. However, the death of the ego usually comes about, not as is commonly supposed through absorption into something or someone else (the beloved, the Cause, God), but through a denial of any form of identification. In other words, the ego exists only in its identifications: get rid of the identifications and you get rid of the ego. Modern philosopher-theologians such as Karl Barth, Paul Tillich, R. Bultmann and Martin Buber, in their efforts to demythologize religion and to establish a concept of man that is both ancient and modern (a fresh formulation of old truths or of the Truth) produce similar arguments. Buber, for instance,

regards man as fully human only in his mutually modifying relationships, which are precisely the hazardous relationships that are often
avoided. In *The Knowledge of Man* Buber writes that, 'Man exists
anthropologically not in his isolation, but in the completeness of
the relation between man and man; what humanity is can be
properly grasped only in vital reciprocity.'[12] In Buber's *I and Thou*
we are told that 'I' cannot exist without 'thou', because each of
these pronouns and the existents to which they refer are components
of an original 'I-thou' unity, etymologically and psychologically.
This is a variant of Heidegger's *Dasein* and of Boss's 'being-in-the-
world'. It means of course that the 'I' does not exist in isolation, yet
—in accordance with De Martino's remarks—cannot realize itself
through mere identification. Likewise the theme of Paul Tillich's
The Courage to Be is the need to progress towards fully-developed
being, in the Heideggerean sense, as the means of apprehending
one's unity with the ground of being. 'Neurosis', he writes, 'is the
way of avoiding non-being by avoiding being.'[13] In other words the
neurotic, fearful of annihilation, codifies his responses—as indeed
almost everyone does to some extent. The openness to experience
recommended by Tillich (which is reminiscent of St Augustine's
injunction, 'Love God and do as you will') is a recurring theme of
all these writers, whether they are theologians, psychologists or
philosophers. All in one way or another are existentialistic and all
seek a fresh mode of unification. Rollo May summarizes the matter
when he writes that, 'Existentialism, in short, is the endeavour to
understand man by cutting below the cleavage between subject and
object which has bedeviled Western thought and science since
shortly after the Renaissance.'[14]

The foregoing paragraphs contain mere samples from a small but
representative selection of authors. A vast number of writers have
recently been expressing similar attitudes, so that here surely is the
modern theme in the West. Now we must tackle the question of
what bearing this theme has upon the contemporary novel. As
always there are two facets, the metaphysical and the ethical. What
sort of a being is man, and how should he behave? We began by
noting that in late Hardy man is out of touch with nature though
governed by nature's laws. His sensibility is a fine organization in a
crude environment. We noted also that in Kafka man is actually
defined by metaphysical and moral perplexity. The only value lies
in the refusal of certainty and the retention of a sense of guilt. To
have been born means to have become an individual; and individuality, separateness from things and people, is itself the crime.
This is the maelstrom from which existential psychologists and
philosophers have been trying to emerge. Their solution, like the
solution of Edgar Allan Poe's mariner in 'A Descent into the

Maelstrom', lies in co-operation with the forces of nature. Individuality, for instance, cannot be a crime because it is the natural condition of modern man, and whatever is, is right. There are no pre-existent canons but only the obligation to discern the true nature of any situation. Morality, as Henry James was beginning to imply in his novels, arises from the fullest awareness. To see rightly is to act rightly; the meaning of a situation shines forth from the situation, and the individual's whole duty is to catch the beams of light.

So, some novelists two or three generations ago dramatized a modern problem to which in more recent years a large number of theorists, whatever their differences of emphasis, have given similar answers. But a good deal of contemporary fiction does not support this new concept of man, and the final stage of our enquiry must be concerned with this discrepancy. Are creative writers now, as so often in the past, ahead of the theorists, more aware of complexities and therefore less optimistic? Alternatively, are novelists in a special, and possibly an inauspicious, situation? Let us approach the answer by first noting some distinguishing features of the contemporary novel.

Many of the more interesting novels of our time fall into one of two opposing categories: the fantastic and the narrowly realistic. Realism—to take this category first—means fidelity to the phenomenal world. The realistic novelist depicts what might very well have happened, but he does so in order to express his interpretation of life. No real-life characters, situations or stories would, without modification, suit his purpose equally well because his interpretation, though true in some sense, would be falsified by adherence to facts. If, for instance, D. H. Lawrence had confined himself to reporting certain facts about Lady Ottoline Morrell instead of inventing the character of Hermione Roddice in *Women in Love*, what he discerned as the true import of Lady Ottoline would not have found adequate expression. As a reporter Lawrence would have failed fully to bring out what Wilhelm Dilthey calls 'the essential in the particular which is the typical'.[15] Similarly, if Thomas Mann had constructed a documentary account of the life and times of his parents and forebears instead of writing the novel, *Buddenbrooks*, his own 'correct' vision of his family would have been destroyed. Likewise, Joyce considered that *A Portrait of the Artist as a Young Man* was truer than *Stephen Hero* partly because it was less factually accurate. Thus 'poetry', according to Aristotle's dictum, is more philosophical than history.

We all realize that it is necessary to make a selection from messy, incoherent facts: most people make a conventional or purblind selection, whereas the great realistic novelist makes a personal selection that turns out to have universal implications. This is because, however little he may be overtly concerned with universalities, he is always driving towards the universal through a serious concern with the world around him and a critical awareness of his own disposition. Such a novelist, being dissatisfied with egotistical, conventional or insular explanations, tries to distil from facts their least assailable meaning.

I have been teasing out truisms as a preliminary to observing that of late many realistic novelists have been content with particulars rather than universals, or, in other words, have been aspiring towards the condition of the reporter, historian or biographer. There seems here and there to be almost an envy of the reporter, and among the reading public there seems to be a preference for him. At the same time actual reporters have been aspiring towards the condition of the novelist. In fact in the past thirty years realistic fiction, adventure stories, popular history, biography and reportage have all been drawing closer together. A few examples should serve to illustrate this tendency.

In the 1940s two non-fiction works of the novelist, John Hersey— *Hiroshima* and *The Wall*—employed novelistic devices to portray real happenings—the day of the first atom bomb and life in the Warsaw ghetto. These excellent books were instances of the higher journalism in that each displayed scrupulous adherence to facts, good writing and formal composition worthy of a novelist. Since that time it has become commonplace for authors to construct absorbing narratives of contemporary events; of assassinations, battles, judicial enquiries, murders, and so on.

But of course it is not only contemporary events that are treated in this (often exhilarating) way: the popular historian likewise gathers up the facts—about Culloden, or about the Somme, or about an incident of the Russian revolution—and makes of them a fascinating tale. Thus Cecil Woodham Smith's *The Reason Why* and *The Great Hunger*, though scholarly expositions of the Charge of the Light Brigade and the Irish troubles of the forties can be read, and presumably usually are read, with the kind of enjoyment that used to be derived only from fiction. If it sounds absurd to say that Cecil Woodham Smith's books—like the two works I have mentioned of John Hersey—fail to be novels only because nothing in them is invented, this, apart from the element of exaggeration, is because invention is not the sole differentia of a novel. A personal interpretation of the world cast in the mould of a long and more or less complicated prose narrative is what really marks the novelist off from the non-novelist who borrows his techniques.

It is not wholly misleading to speak of the novelist as reporter, or the reporter as novelist. Norman Mailer's *Armies of the Night*,

Miami and the Siege of Chicago and *A Fire on the Moon*, may reasonably be spoken of in this way, somewhat as his *Marilyn* might encourage talk of the novelist as biographer. Truman Capote, of course, went so far as to call *In Cold Blood* a 'non-fiction novel', though in fact his account of the Kansas farm murders of 1959 was merely (but skilfully) written in the manner of a novel. It is very much to the point that Capote should seek to minimize the difference between fiction and reportage and should in his book eschew the novelist's private vision.

Yet another aspect of this literary situation is of course the proliferation of thrillers, which are popular precisely because they avoid the improbabilities formerly regarded as unavoidable in such works. For many years Eric Ambler's production of realistic adventure novels was not impressively emulated by other British writers, until Frederick Forsyth's *The Day of the Jackal* was published in 1971. Forsyth has successfully carried pseudo-documentation to its extreme and a host of other writers are following suit with convincingly detailed stories of C.I.A. conspiracies, Middle Eastern intrigues, Mafia feuds, mercenary-aided uprisings and the like.

The distinction between real reportage, such as William Manchester's *Death of a President* and imitation reportage, such as Forsyth's *The Dogs of War*, is presumably clear to nearly all readers, yet for many, I imagine, the distinction scarcely matters. And there may be people who fancy that *The French Connection*, for instance, is a novel, and that *The Sicilian Conspiracy* recounts actual events.

Reflecting on this phase of narrow realism, we can see the prophetic nature of a remark given to the hero of Aldous Huxley's *Time Must Have a Stop* (1945):

> In the past there was an age of Shakespeare, of Voltaire, of Dickens. Ours is the age, not of any poet or thinker or novelist, but of the Document. Our Representative Man is the travelling newspaper correspondent, who dashes off a best seller between assignments.[16]

Of course many contemporary documentations are, like William Manchester's book, meticulously researched rather than dashed off, but this is a minor point. The main point is the preference for fact or pseudo-fact over obvious fiction. And it may be because ours is not the age of any poet, novelist or thinker that some novelists have shifted as far away as possible from what Huxley ironically calls the 'Document'. For fantasy, the second distinguishing category of our period of the novel, is also amply stocked.

I do not seriously suggest that many authors have abandoned

realism, turning instead to sophisticated fables, to science fiction or to weird apocalyptic tales, simply in order to distinguish their products from those of the reporter. But a fear that the world is growing tired of imaginative literature may sometimes have fostered zealous displays of the power of the imagination. After all, the writer of serious fiction builds his life on the supposition that the imagination working through the written word is—apart, possibly, from religion—the best way of making sense of things. Such a writer is now facing the fact that fewer and fewer people want or need to make sense of things in this way. Many people, indeed, seem to have what Marshall McLuhan calls 'tribal sensory balance', a capacity to respond to diverse stimuli without desiring to reflect upon their individual experiences through the medium of careful verbal constructions. Perhaps it is partly for this reason that some writers have attempted to match in fiction the same effects of disorganization, the same fusion of meanings into barely translatable images.

Novels of this type proclaim the primacy of the imagination: they implicitly maintain that the mind must not be fettered by the material world, by what the senses perceive and by what experience teaches us is probable. We have to allow for, on the one hand, the usual enjoyment of fancy for its own sake and, on the other hand, suggestions that the world has become too senseless for realism to cope with. Fancy for its own sake (though informed by traditional moral values) is the characteristic of such works as J. R. R. Tolkien's *The Hobbit* and *The Lord of the Rings* and Richard Adams's *Watership Down*. But it is the other kind of modern fantasy, the fantasy of moral bewilderment, that I wish to discuss.

Superficially it might be said that such fiction in its modern form began as a response to the Second World War and particularly to nuclear weapons. Compare *Hiroshima*, written by a man who went around the hospitals and talked to survivors, with Aldous Huxley's *Ape and Essence*, a fantasy-response published in 1948. Hersey's book concludes with a question about the morality of dropping the bomb, whereas Huxley's book expresses his fear (not his expectation) that the future could be one of total bestiality. It is interesting that the initial reaction to the bomb of one writer, who, despite *Brave New World*, *After Many a Summer* and *Island*, was not greatly drawn to fantasy, should be a flight into the grotesque, the ghoulish, the neo-gothic.

For the most part, however, novelists' treatment of the war remained more or less realistic (Mailer, James Jones, Irwin Shaw) until it became the subject of satirical fantasy in Joseph Heller's *Catch-22*. On the face of it here is no moral bewilderment but an unqualified assertion that war is farcically evil. The hero, Yossarian, can do nothing of value except escape from the army air corps, as he finally does. In a sense, though, the novel does express perplexity, because Heller—as is perhaps the prerogative of the satirist—just throws up his hands at what he regards as the monstrous futility of the war. Of course fantasy is highly effective as propaganda and Heller's novel is anti-military (not just anti-militarist) propaganda, but its unrealistic nature can be overlooked, even while it is theoretically acknowledged, by the young or the evasive. Of other, more fantastical works, dealing not with the forties but with the later social scene something similar may be said.

What, for instance, are we to make of Anthony Burgess's *A Clockwork Orange*? The hero, Alex, informs us in sprightly argot of his pleasure in beating people up and his identical pleasure in listening to great music. (Listening with great joy to Mozart's 'Jupiter' Symphony, he daydreams about grinding his boots into people's faces.) Alex is arrested for murdering an old woman and after a spell in prison is conditioned, briefly but effectively, to respond to violence in the approved way—that is, with squeamishness and disgust. He is released as a rather ennervated eighteen-year-old, the pride of the progressivists, contemplating a quiet, joyless life. But his parents are indifferent to. him; he is beaten up by policemen (his old friends) and he attempts suicide by jumping from a window. However, shock and injuries restore him to his former, happy, vicious self.

Burgess is probably saying that violence is a concomitant of vitality and that it is wrong forcibly to eradicate the bad. But the mere fact that this novel is a fantasy prevents the author from representing real-life details, against which background alone the moral problem that he raises could be properly explored. And here we come to the heart of the matter. Fantasy, a roundabout way of commenting on the real world, is properly employed in the expression of assured and widely-held values, but once the values are in doubt fantasy becomes an unsuitable vehicle. Sir Thomas Malory, Spenser, the Brothers Grimm, even modern fabulists such as Orwell or C. S. Lewis, all have no doubt that, for instance, courage is admirable and treachery to be deplored, and therefore they engage in the age-old task of teaching delightfully. Such authors and their readers know perfectly well that treachery should be eschewed in life, as in the simplified tale. As people grow less and less sure of what constitutes treachery (the clear tribal code gives way to the individual conscience) they begin to write or read realistic novels in which the intricacies of actual decisions are imitated. At the point when the very wrongness of treachery begins to be questioned authors should become more not less realistic, because a simplified story can neither state nor solve the problem except in hazy and speculative terms. Thus modern fantasy lends itself to evasion.

If Burgess was evasive in his novel (as I think he was), Norman Mailer's attitude is indeterminate in *Why Are We in Vietnam?* On Mailer's presentation the dominant strain in American males is one of crude sexual aggression, but the novel offers no corrective to this condition. Similarly, this author's most recent novel, *An American Dream*, is a portrait of scarcely mitigated evil, somewhat Jacobean in its strange acceptance, if not exaltation, of bestialities. But the hero, Rojack, is intended to be admirable in his surrender to dark forces: it is as if he rises above the other characters through a greater, braver *rapport* with the evil tendencies of the age. The book raises to a higher power the stock themes and personages of a thousand films: the gangster's girl who loves the hero and is killed, the weary homicide detective, the abrupt violence, the wailing sirens, the finale in the desert near Las Vegas. Of course Mailer in this novel, as in *Why Are We in Vietnam?*, was embodying his understanding of the American psyche, but it is interesting that in order to do this he found it necessary to incorporate fantastical elements. The implicit assumption is that detailed observation of actual people in actual situations (the procedure of Tolstoy or of George Eliot) would not yield up the truth, since our behaviour arises from a subterranean fantasy-world. In one respect this belief is in the Freudian tradition, and it particularly matches the arguments of some neo-Freudians that the unconscious is largely composed of fantasies,[17] but Freud's own concern was to regulate the power of the unconscious, whereas Mailer seems to be advocating a surrender of reason.

Nevertheless, a genuine concern with the condition of contemporary America is apparent in *An American Dream* and for this reason the novel is plainly superior to some other nihilistic fantasies of our time. Indeed, the important difference that emerges from a consideration of modern fantasy-fiction is the age-old difference between the serious (including, of course, the serio-comic) and the flippant or evasive. The right way for a critic to assess the value of recent fantasies is to ask how well they illustrate the everyday world, no matter how far removed from the everyday world their contents apparently are. Thus—to give vent to some unsupported opinions about a few diverse works of the last twenty years or so—I would say that we should look searchingly at Lawrence Durrell's *Alexandria Quartet* and William Golding's *Pincher Martin* rather than revering them because of their power and pessimism, and that we should not be dazzled by the brilliance of Nabokov's *Pale Fire*. On the other hand we should applaud the readiness of Iris Murdoch to take up severe moral and philosophical challenges in her novels, even if by

117

bizarre means, and we should pay careful attention to Kingsley Amis's contemplation of the nature of evil in *The Green Man* and his treatment of pain and loss in *The Anti-Death League*. There are many other fantasies of recent years about which one is less sure, including a good deal of ingenious and highly regarded science fiction.

These remarks about the contemporary novel have so far given a partial picture, consisting of two rival tendencies: between these tendencies lies the range of fiction that is realistic without being narrowly so. I have omitted all those novelists who are endeavouring, just as Tolstoy and George Eliot and Henry James endeavoured, to compose a picture of man out of direct, intricate observations of the real world. Such novelists (Iris Murdoch, Angus Wilson and Bernard Malamud are clear examples) are carrying on a tradition without being, in an excessively limited sense, traditional. In saying this I am not making the familiar distinction between experimentalism and traditionalism, because the vital thing—the drive towards universality through accurate observations of the particular—seems to me unconnected with the degree of experimentation. However, the interesting truth is that it is just these traditionally realistic novelists who most clearly express what I have called, with reference to psychology and philosophy, the 'modern theme'.

These novelists rather than the makers of either fantasy or documentary are carrying forward the modern movement, for the vital feature of modernism in the arts has not been experimentalism as such but the attempt to reach a fresh understanding of human nature. In the earlier years of the century Freud and Jung, as much as any novelist, poet or playwright, enlarged the concept of man. Although many of their hypotheses may prove to have been false, their contribution in cultural terms amounted to a necessary accommodation of human characteristics that it had long been thought desirable to eliminate. They each maintained that spirit and flesh were interdependent, so that valid spiritual aspirations could not be thwarted (as, for example, in Hardy) by the laws of the universe.

But the scientism of Freud, if not of Jung, made it inevitable that such an understanding remained theoretical, while in Jung alongside or surrounding the many convincing insights there is what many have found to be a less convincing modification of old myths. Lawrence's contribution included railing against science and against 'ghastly knowers' (of whom Freud was one of the ghastliest), but most importantly consisted of asserting that each individual should strive to grow in his own way: should aim for a certain 'fullness of being', which, however, could not be contemplated in advance. Thus Lawrence helped both to restore individuality and to link people more firmly with other forms of life, since all living things, he insisted, exhibited the same principle of growth.

Virginia Woolf and Proust, and after them the neo-Freudians, concentrated on a different—though not necessarily an opposed—way of achieving individuality. To them personal identity, and concomitantly a sense of unity with others, was secured through accurate awareness of one's moment-by-moment perceptions. Identity was realized to the extent that pre-conceptions were laid aside and self-identifications broken down.

The differences between Lawrence, Virginia Woolf and Proust, and between any of these authors and the existentialists who followed them, are enormous and—in view of the practice among critics of producing close individual studies—are not likely to be underestimated. The difficulty may rather be in convincing anyone that these diverse writers have anything in common. But from a historical point of view they have in common something of the greatest importance—a destruction of 'essentialism', the belief that an individual has a sort of pre-existent self of which his behaviour is a more or less accurate manifestation. What we have noted in all of them—Lawrence as much as Sartre, Virginia Woolf as much as the existential psychologist, Boss—is a transformation of the notion of 'character' into a vision of successive states of being. Virginia Woolf talked of the 'key self' and Lawrence spoke of the 'spontaneous life-motive', but their very concern with these amalgamating factors reveals an existentialistic awareness. It reveals also a recognition of the need to re-unite the individual with his environment, without pressing into service some general doctrine of unity. The way is through responsible self-choice and disinterested personal perception rather than through faith and myth.

A barely separable part of this development has been the moral question, for clearly, a discovery that individuals are always—as Boss puts it—'out in the world', deriving their very identity from their specific relationships and ideally relying as much as possible upon their own observations, involves a kind of moral relativism. It is this fact, presumably, that leads some novelists to be narrowly realistic and others to be either irresponsibly or despairingly fantastical. Members of the former category subordinate themselves to the state of affairs they are describing, while members of the latter exalt their own fancies over reality. The first group demeans mind (if we can still call it that) and the second group tries to confer upon mind powers it has not got. So we have either materialism or solipsism.

These, then, are regular types of unsatisfactory response to an exceedingly challenging situation. The right response may be expressed as the attempt to prove Dostoevsky wrong when he caused Ivan Karamazov to declare that if God did not exist and there were no after life, everything would be lawful.[18] The attempt in the novelists I have earlier discussed at length, and among some contemporary novelists, is to extract meaning and value from particular situations. It is increasingly contended that false values and bad impulses are effects rather than causes of deficiencies in perception. The bad is consequent upon some narrowing or blunting of the natural vision. To say this is not in the least to echo Rousseau's remark that, 'Everything is good when it leaves the hands of the Creator of things; everything degenerates in the hands of man.'[19] In Rousseau, whose attitudes still find abundant expression, man is alienated from nature by civilization, by institutions, by urban living and by the growth of artificial needs. But I am now discussing an obfuscation of the natural vision that has been thrown into relief as well as produced by modern conditions. (Actual, as opposed to noble, savages were thoroughly communalized.) A conception, a categorization, is borrowed from others or dreamed up by oneself and through inertia is allowed to blot out the richness of actuality. What this might almost amount to saying is not that there are no general laws, but that there is only one general law: cultivate an efficient perception of reality. Nature is paramount, not in the old scientific or quasi-scientific sense, according to which man was a neutral observer who could do no more than observe what was objectively there, but in a quasi-Einsteinian sense in which the position of the observer has also to be taken into account.

On this basis there need be no inevitable alienation, which must be the result only of exalting mind over matter in the wrong way.[20] There certainly need be no sense of a 'Fall', of man as 'fallen' into the material world, while his spirit truly belongs elsewhere. Likewise there need be no pessimism, but probably instead a sort of meliorism, accompanied sporadically by joy.

It could also be recognized that people are creative by nature and not as a result of fluke or fortune's favour. The bad is that which confounds creativity, a conclusion that should lead not to indiscipline but to a disciplined rejection of the spurious, of whatever, in fact, crumbles before a discriminating awareness. Creativity and responsibility obviously go hand in hand, so that any device for attributing one's proclivities to an external agency—to God, to the devil, to the 'system', to the local culture, to parental influences, to instincts or even to one's incorrigible 'self'—should be rejected. On this basis it might reasonably be argued that the 'good' hero in a contemporary realistic novel should be one who behaves, or comes to realize that he should behave, in accordance with these principles. His problem will be not to gain the kind of absolute freedom that some people dream of, but to recognize the freedom of necessity, a kind of creative manipulation of the social world within the limits of natural law. It follows that the social world itself must be faithfully presented, or at least faithfully borne in mind, by the author, so that the characters occupy some focal point in a life-like complex of people and events. Something like these sentiments has been well expressed by Iris Murdoch (in the course of a polemic against fictions that exhibit 'free' individuals in grossly simplified social contexts).

Reality is not a given whole. An understanding of this, a respect for the contingent, is essential to imagination as opposed to fantasy. Our sense of form, which is an aspect of our desire for consolation, can be a danger to our sense of reality as a rich receding background. Against the consolations of form, the clear crystalline work, the simplified fantasy-myth, we must pit the now so unfashionable naturalistic idea of character.

Real people are destructive of myth, contingency is destructive of fantasy, and opens the way for imagination. Think of the Russians, those great masters of the contingent. Too much contingency, of course, may turn out into journalism. Literature must always represent a battle between real people and images; and what it requires now is a much stronger and more complex conception of the former.[21]

I think that Miss Murdoch's comparison in the last clause is not between what we ought to have and what we now have, but between what we ought to have and what literature has throughout its history manifested. If so, this in effect is what this study has been leading up to saying. The development from the days of Hardy and early Freud should be seen not as an excuse or a need to turn away from what the nineteenth-century realists attempted, but rather as a means of returning to their kind of struggle with an expanded—and continually expanding—vision of man. Fixities dissolve, horizons recede; the individual and his world grow more amorphous. The whole effort of such novelists and thinkers as I have chiefly dealt with has been to stand firm while not denying the various kinds of dissolution. Their hardly maintained stability has pointed the way to a new accommodation of man to nature. What the present situation exacts is a transformation of our sense of exposure into a sense of dawning possibilities.

Notes

Introduction: 'Convergent Roads'

1. Virginia Woolf, 'Mr Bennett and Mrs Brown', *Collected Essays* Vol. 1, Hogarth Press, 1966, p. 320. (Originally a paper read in 1924)
2. Gordon S. Haight, *George Eliot*, Oxford University Press, 1968, p. 496
3. *The Standard Edition of the Complete Psychological Works of Sigmund Freud* (ed. James Strachey), Hogarth Press, Vol. 19, p. 15
4. If it should be asked how unconscious forces can collaborate with consciousness, the answer, it seems, is that they do so by symbolic means—principally in art, religion, dreams, fantasies, mandalas.
5. Helen Merrell Lynd, *On Shame and the Search for Identity*, Harcourt Brace & World, New York, 1958, p. 14

Chapter 1: 'The Burden of Consciousness'

1. Émile Zola, 'The Naturalist Novel' (1893), *The Nineteenth Century Novel* (ed. A. Kettle), Heinemann, 1972, p. 317
2. *The Return of the Native*, Chapter 2
3. I refer only to *The Return of the Native*, though this remark is with qualifications also applicable to Hardy's last two novels. It does not apply to such novels as *The Woodlanders* and *Far From the Madding Crowd*, while Hardy's attitude to nature or external necessity is, I think, ambivalent in *The Mayor of Casterbridge*.
4. *Tess of the D'Urbervilles*, Chapter 39
5. *Jude the Obscure*, Part 6, Chapter 3
6. Sigmund Freud, *Introductory Lectures on Psycho-Analysis* (tr. Joan Riviere), Allen & Unwin, 1922, pp. 17f.
7. *idem*, p. 16
8. *idem*, p. 17
9. It is possible, as Lionel Trilling has shown ('Freud and Literature', *The Liberal Imagination*), to see Freud as the heir to countless generations of romantic artists, but Freud's systematic account of the dependence of the 'highest' upon the 'lowest' nevertheless deserves to be called 'revolutionary'.
10. Leon Edel, *Henry James: The Conquest of London, 1870–1883*, Hart-Davis, 1962, p. 435
11. *The Portrait of a Lady*, Chapter 6
12. A. J. Geurard, *Conrad the Novelist*, Harvard University Press, Mass., 1958, p. 7
13. Sigmund Freud, *Beyond the Pleasure Principle* (tr. James Strachey), Hogarth Press, 1950, p. 86. (First published in German, 1920)
14. *Lord Jim*, Chapter 20

15. Sigmund Freud, *The Future of an Illusion*, The Standard Edition, Vol. 21, pp. 55f.
16. Franz Kafka, *Dearest Father* (tr. Ernst Kaiser and Eithne Wilkins), Schocken Books, New York, 1954, p. 66
17. Sigmund Freud, *Totem and Taboo* (tr. James Strachey), Routledge, 1950, p. 73
18. Thomas Mann, *Past Masters and other Papers* (tr. H. T. Lowe-Porter), Secker & Warburg, 1933, p. 198
19. Thomas Mann, 'Goethe and Tolstoy', *Three Essays* (tr. H. T. Lowe-Porter), New York, 1929
20. *The Magic Mountain* (tr. H. T. Lowe-Porter), English Edition, 1928, p. 729
21. Thomas Mann, *Past Masters, ed. cit.*, p. 178

Chapter 2: 'The Nature of the Unconscious'

1. Sigmund Freud, 'The Unconscious', The Standard Edition, Vol. 14, p. 187
2. Sigmund Freud, *The Interpretation of Dreams*, Second Part, The Standard Edition, Vol. 5, p. 608
3. Later, in *Beyond the Pleasure Principle* (1919), Freud took account of disagreeable dreams of the 'repetition-compulsion' type, which had nothing to do with wish-fulfilment but, he concluded, were attempts to master an unpleasant experience.
4. 'Ulysses', *The Spirit in Man, Art and Literature, The Collected Works of C. G. Jung*, (tr. S. M. Dell), Routledge, 1959, Vol. 15
5. Frank Budgen, *James Joyce and the Making of 'Ulysses'* (int. Clive Hart), Oxford University Press, 1972, p. 18. (First published 1934)
6. *op. cit.*, p. 657
7. D. H. Lawrence, *Fantasia of the Unconscious* and *Psychoanalysis and the Unconscious*, Penguin Books, 1971, pp. 212f. (First published by Wm. Heinemann, 1923)
8. *The Rainbow*, Chapter 15
9. *op. cit.*, p. 15
10. Abraham H. Maslow, *Motivation and Personality*, 2nd edition, Harper & Row, New York, 1954, p. 102

Chapter 3: 'The Living Self'

1. D. H. Lawrence, *The Collected Letters* (ed. Harry T. Moore), Heinemann, 1962, Vol. 2, p. 938
2. Jolande Jacobi, *The Psychology of C. G. Jung*, Routledge, 1968, p. 121. (1st edition, 1948)
3. D. H. Lawrence, *Fantasia of the Unconscious, ed. cit.*, p. 100
4. *The Letters of D. H. Lawrence* (ed. Aldous Huxley), Heinemann, 1932, pp. 100f.
5. *op. cit.*, p. 46
6. However, Jungians regard marrying a woman who corresponds to one's Anima as a risky proceeding, and this may be borne out by the subsequent history of Lawrence's relationship with Frieda. Very shortly before he died Lawrence is reported to have told Aldous Huxley

that Frieda's attitudes and personality were killing him.
7. *Letters of Aldous Huxley* (ed. Grover Smith), Chatto & Windus, 1964, Letter No. 780, pp. 831f.
8. F. R. Leavis, *D. H. Lawrence Novelist*, Chatto & Windus, 1955, p. 169
9. D. H. Lawrence, 'Reflections on the Death of a Porcupine', *Selected Essays*, Penguin Books, 1950, p. 66

Chapter 4: 'The Search for Identity'
1. English translation by Roger Shattuck, *Proust*, Fontana, 1974, p. 169
2. *Swann's Way* (tr. C. K. Scott Moncrieff), Chatto & Windus illustrated edition, 1966, p. 58
3. *Mrs Dalloway*, Hogarth Press, 1931, p. 203
4. *The Waves*, Hogarth Press, 1931, p. 203
5. *Orlando*, Hogarth Press, 1931, p. 279
6. See *A Writer's Diary*, Hogarth Press, 1953, p. 72
7. Perhaps it is necessary to comment that Freud did not lose his sense of the importance of the unconscious, but having discovered the prevalence and significance of ego conflicts, concentrated upon investigating the ego.
8. See Jean-Paul Sartre, *Words*, Penguin Books, 1967, p. 115: ... 'since I had discovered the world through language, for a long time I mistook language for the world', and, p. 156: ... 'I confused things with their names.'
9. D. H. Lawrence, 'Study of Thomas Hardy', *Selected Literary Criticism* (ed. Anthony Beal), Heinemann, 1955, p. 222

Chapter 5: 'Attack on the Unconscious'
1. Henri Bergson, *Time and Free Will* (tr. F. L. Pogson), Allen & Unwin 1971, p. 219. (First published, 1910)
2. See above, p. 35
3. See for example John Passmore's *A Hundred Years of Philosophy*, Penguin Books, 1968, p. 466. 'Professional philosophers, for the most part, dismiss it [existentialism] with a contemptuous shrug.' Also, p. 490, 'Sartre in English-speaking countries is not uncommonly dismissed as a pamphleteer, a "literary man", interesting, perhaps, as illustrating the decadence of post-war European culture, but of no consequence as a philosopher.'
4. Jean-Paul Sartre, *Being and Nothingness* (tr. Hazel E. Barnes), Methuen, 1974, p. 54. (Original edition, *L'Etre et le Néant*, Paris, 1943)
5. An interesting discussion of this aspect of Sartre's attack on the unconscious occurs in Lionel Trilling's *Sincerity and Authenticity* (1972), pp. 144–50. Trilling points out that Sartre's arguments are directed towards Freud's earlier formulations and ignore Freud's later view that part of the ego itself is unconscious and behaves like the repressed. However, Trilling does not refute Sartre's argument so much as maintain that Freud moved towards a recognition of the sort of inauthenticity that Sartre is concerned with. To Trilling an un-

conscious consciousness is merely a terminological contradiction but to Sartre it is the root of the moral problem.

6. R. D. Laing, *Self and Others*, Penguin Books, 1971, p. 36
7. Jean-Paul Sartre, *Existentialism and Humanism* (tr. P. Mairet), Methuen, 1948, p. 42. (Originally *Existentialisme est un Humanisme*, Paris, 1946)
8. In *Words*, Sartre writes: 'Some years ago it was pointed out to me that the characters in my plays and novels make their decisions suddenly and in crises—that, for instance, it takes only a moment for Orestes in Les Mouches to achieve his conversion. By Jove: that is because I make them in my own image; not as I am, I dare say, but as I have wanted to be.' *Words*, p. 148
9. Iris Murdoch, *Sartre*, Fontana, 1967, p. 7. (First published by Bowes & Bowes, 1953)
10. Norman Mailer, *The Naked and the Dead*, Allan Wingate, p. 156
11. *op. cit.*, p. 29
12. Saul Bellow, *Dangling Man*, Weidenfeld & Nicolson, 1946, pp. 127f. (First published 1944)
13. *Being and Nothingness*, ed. cit., p. 89
14. *idem*, pp. 566f.

Chapter 6: 'A New Synthesis'

1. See Bertrand Russell, *History of Western Philosophy*, p. 550: Descartes's philosophy 'brought to completion, or very near to completion, the dualism of mind and matter which began with Plato . . .'
2. T. H. Huxley, 'On the Hypothesis that Animals are Automata, and its History'. Lecture delivered to British Association, 1874. Quoted in *Industrialization and Culture* (ed. Harvie, Martin and Scharf), Macmillan, 1970, p. 212
3. Gilbert Ryle, *The Concept of Mind*, Hutchinson, 1949, p. 27
4. John MacMurray, *The Self as Agent*, Faber, 1957, p. 21
5. *idem*, p. 91
6. *idem*, p. 118
7. Karl Jaspers, *General Psychopathology* (tr. J. Hoenig and M. W. Hamilton), Regnery, Chicago, 1963, p. 350. (Original edition *Allgemeine Psychopathologie*, 1913)
8. Medard Boss, *Psychoanalysis and Daseinsanalysis* (tr. Ludwig B. Lefebre), Basic Books, New York, 1963, p. 30
9. *Reason and Violence*, written jointly by Laing and D. G. Cooper, is in fact a brilliant précis of three of Sartre's works, *Saint Genet, Search for a Method* and *The Problem of Method*.
10. D. T. Suzuki, *Zen Buddhism and Psychoanalysis* (ed. Erich Fromm), Souvenir Press, 1974, pp. 9 and 20. (Original edition Harper & Row, New York, 1970)
11. *idem*, pp. 164f.
12. Martin Buber, *The Knowledge of Man* (tr. Maurice Friedman and Ronald Gregor Smith), Allen & Unwin, 1965, p. 84
13. Paul Tillich, *The Courage to Be*, Collins, 1962, p. 71

14. *Existence* (ed. Rollo May, Ernest Angel, Henri F. Ellenburger), Basic Books, New York, 1958, p. 11
15. Quoted in Kurt Müller-Vollmer's *Towards a Phenomenological Theory of Literature*, Mouton & Co., The Hague, 1963
16. Aldous Huxley, *Time Must Have a Stop*, Chatto & Windus, 1966, Chapter 30
17. See, for example, *Developments in Psycho-Analysis* (ed. Joan Riviere), Hogarth Press, 1952
18. *The Brothers Karamazov*, Book II, Chapter 6
19. Jean-Jacques Rousseau, *Émile*, p. 1
20. This brisk remark overlooks the complexity of some analyses of alienation, notably Marx's, but it is intended to glance at Marx's criticisms of Hegel and Feuerbach in the 'Theses on Feuerbach'. Marx contends that the 'dualistic materialism' of Feuerbach, no less than the idealism of Hegel, gives primacy to the mind (the concept in Hegel, the 'theoretical attitude' in Feuerbach) and therefore fails to solve the problem of alienation.
21. Iris Murdoch, 'Against Dryness', *Encounter*, January 1961, p. 20

Bibliography

When a book is available in Britain and America, the UK edition precedes the American.
Easily accessible editions of the novels are listed below, but many are available in other editions as well.

ADLER, Alfred   *The Neurotic Constitution*, Kegan Paul, Trench, Trubner, 1921; Books for Libraries Press, 1972
ADAMS, Richard   *Watership Down*, William Collins, 1972; Macmillan, 1974
AMIS, Kingsley   *The Anti-Death League*, Victor Gollancz, 1966; Penguin, 1975
   The Green Man, Jonathan Cape, 1969; Harcourt Brace, 1970
BEDFORD, Sybille   *Aldous Huxley*, Vol. 1, Chatto & Windus, 1973; Knopf, 1974
BELLOW, Saul   *The Adventures of Augie March*, Weidenfeld & Nicolson, 1954; Viking, 1953
   Dangling Man, Weidenfeld & Nicolson 1972; Vanguard
   Herzog, Weidenfeld & Nicolson, 1965; Viking, 1964
   Sammler's Planet, Weidenfeld & Nicolson 1970; Viking, 1970
   Seize the Day, Weidenfeld & Nicolson, 1957; Viking, 1961
   The Victim, Penguin, 1966; Vanguard
BERGSON, Henri   *Matter and Memory* (tr. Paul & Palmer), Allen & Unwin, 1911; Humanities Press, 1970 (Original edition, 1896)
   Time and Free Will (tr. F. L. Pogson), Allen & Unwin, 1971 (Original edition, 1910)
BERNE, Eric   *Games People Play*, André Deutsch, 1966; Grove, 1964
BOSS, Medard   *Psychoanalysis and Daseinsanalysis* (tr. Ludwig B. Lefebre), Basic Books, New York, 1963
BRADLEY, F. H.   *Appearance and Reality*, Oxford University Press, 1930
BUBER, Martin   *I and Thou* (tr. W. Kaufman), T. & T. Clark, Edinburgh, 1971; Scribner, 1970
BUDGEN, Frank   *James Joyce and the Making of 'Ulysses'* (int. Clive Hart, Oxford University Press, 1972; Indiana University Press, 1960 (First published 1934)
BURGESS, Anthony   *A Clockwork Orange*, William Heinemann, 1962; Ballantine, 1971
CAMUS, Albert   *The Myth of Sisyphus*, Hamish Hamilton, 1955; Knopf, 1955
CAPOTE, Truman   *In Cold Blood*, Hamish Hamilton, 1966; Random House, 1966

CONRAD, Joseph *Heart of Darkness*, Bantam, 1969
Lord Jim, Pan, 1975; Macmillan, 1966
The Nigger of the Narcissus, J. M. Dent, 1961; Macmillan, 1962
DICKENS, Charles *Great Expectations*, William Collins, 1961; Macmillan, 1962
DOSTOEVSKY, Fydor *The Brothers Karamazov*, (int. Edward Garnett), J. M. Dent, 1936; Bantam, 1970
DURRELL, Lawrence *The Alexandria Quartet*, Faber & Faber; Dutton
EDEL, Leon *Henry James: The Conquest of London 1870–1883*, Hart-Davis, 1962; Lippincott, 1962
ELIOT, George *Daniel Deronda*, J. M. Dent, 1964; Penguin, 1975
FAIRBAIRN, W. R. D. *Psychoanalytic Studies of the Personality*, Routledge & Kegan Paul, London and New York, 1952
FORSTER, E. M. *Howards End*, Edward Arnold, 1973; Random House, 1954
FORSYTH, Frederick *The Day of the Jackal*, Hutchinson, 1971; Bantam, 1972
The Dogs of War, Hutchinson, 1974; Viking, 1974
FREUD, Anna *The Ego and the Mechanisms of Defence*, The Hogarth Press, Revised Edition (tr. Cecil Baines), 1966; International Universities Press, 1967 (Original edition, 1936)
FREUD, Sigmund *Beyond the Pleasure Principle*, The Standard Edition of the Complete Psychological Works of Sigmund Freud (ed. James Strachey), Vol. 18, The Hogarth Press, 1950; Norton, 1975
The Future of an Illusion, The Standard Edition, Vol. 21
The Interpretation of Dreams, The Standard Edition, Vol. 5
Introductory Lectures on Psycho-Analysis, The Standard Edition, Vol. 19
Introductory Lectures on Psycho-Analysis (tr. Joan Riviere), Allen & Unwin, 1922
Totem and Taboo (tr. James Strachey), Routledge & Kegan Paul, 1950
'The Unconscious', The Standard Edition, Vol. 14
FROMM, Erich (ed.) *Zen Buddhism and Psychoanalysis*, Souvenir Press, 1974; Harper & Row, 1970
GALSWORTHY, John *The Forsyte Saga*, William Heinemann, 1922; Scribner, 1933
GOLDING, William *Pincher Martin*, Faber & Faber, 1954; Harcourt Brace, 1968
GUERARD, Albert J. *Conrad the Novelist*, Harvard University Press, Cambridge, Massachusetts, 1958
HAIGHT, Gordon S. *George Eliot*, Oxford University Press, Oxford and New York, 1968
HARDY, Thomas *Far From the Madding Crowd*, Macmillan, 1965; Bantam, 1967
Jude the Obscure, Macmillan, 1949; Bobbs-Merrill, 1972
The Mayor of Casterbridge, Macmillan 1975; NAL
The Return of the Native, Macmillan, 1964; Norton, 1969
Tess of the D'Urbervilles, Macmillan, 1964; Norton, 1966
The Woodlanders, Macmillan, 1963; St Martin, 1887

HEIDEGGER, Martin *Being and Time* (tr. J. Macquarrie and E. Robinson), Oxford University Press, 1973; Harper & Row, 1962 (Original edition, 1927)

HELLER, Joseph *Catch—22*, Jonathan Cape, 1962; Simon & Schuster, 1961

HEMINGWAY, Ernest *Across the River into the Trees*, Jonathan Cape, 1950; Scribner, 1950

A Farewell to Arms, Jonathan Cape, 1966; Scribner, 1967

For Whom the Bell Tolls, Jonathan Cape, 1941; Scribner, 1940

In Our Time, Scribner, New York, 1930

The Old Man and the Sea, Jonathan Cape, 1955; Scribner, 1960

The Sun Also Rises, Pan, 1972; Scribner, 1926

To Have and Have Not, Penguin, 1969; Scribner, 1937

HERSEY, John *Hiroshima*, Penguin, 1972; Bantam

The Wall, Hamish Hamilton, 1950

HUXLEY, Aldous *After Many a Summer*, Chatto & Windus, 1968; Harper & Row, 1965

Ape and Essence, Chatto & Windus, 1967; Harper & Row, 1972

Brave New World, Chatto & Windus, 1967; Harper & Row, 1969

Island, Chatto & Windus, 1962; Harper & Row, 1962

Letters of Aldous Huxley (ed. Grover Smith), Chatto & Windus, 1964

Time Must Have a Stop, Chatto & Windus, 1966; Harper & Row, 1965

HUXLEY, T. H. 'On the Hypothesis that Animals are Automata, and its History', *Industrialization and Culture* (ed. Harvie, Martin and Scharf), Macmillan, 1970 (Original Lecture, 1874)

JACOBI, Jolande *The Psychology of C. G. Jung*, Routledge & Kegan Paul, 1948; Yale University Press, 1963

JAMES, Henry *The Ambassadors*, Bodley Head, 1970, Norton, 1974

Daisy Miller, Bodley Head, 1974; Airmont, 1968

The Golden Bowl, Methuen, 1963; Penguin, 1973

The Portrait of a Lady, Oxford University Press, 1947; Houghton Mifflin, 1956

The Princess Casamassima, Harper & Row, New York, 1975

The Turn of the Screw, Bodley Head, 1974; Norton, 1967

Washington Square, William Heinemann, 1970; Thomas Crowell, 1970

What Maisie Knew, Bodley Head, 1969; Doubleday

The Wings of the Dove, Penguin, Harmondsworth and New York, 1971

JASPERS, Karl *General Psychopathology* (tr. J. Hoenig and M. W. Hamilton), Regnery, Chicago, 1963 (Original edition, 1913)

JOYCE, James *A Portrait of the Artist as a Young Man*, Jonathan Cape, 1956; Viking, 1964

Finnegans Wake, Faber & Faber, 1950; Viking, 1959

Stephen Hero, Jonathan Cape, 1956; New Directions, 1969

Ulysses, The Bodley Head, 1960; Random House

JUNG, C. G. *The Archetypes and the Collective Unconscious*, Collected Works, Vol. 9 (tr. R. F. C. Hull), Routledge & Kegan Paul; Princeton University Press

The Integration of the Personality (tr. Stanley M. Dell), Kegan Paul, Trench, Trubner, 1940

Modern Man in Search of a Soul, Kegan Paul, 1928; Harcourt Brace, 1955
Psychology of the Unconscious, Kegan Paul, 1916
The Spirit in Man, Art and Literature, Collected Works, Vol. 15, 1966
Symbols of Transformation, Collected Works, Vol. 5, 1956
KAFKA, Franz *The Castle* (tr. W. and E. Muir), Secker & Warburg, 1953; Knopf, 1954
Dearest Father (tr. Ernest Kaiser and Eithne Wilkins), Schocken Books, New York, 1954
Diaries 1910–1913 (ed. Max Brod; tr. Joseph Kresh), Secker & Warburg, 1948; Schocken, 1948
Diaries 1914–1923 (ed. Max Brod; tr. Martin Greenberg), Secker & Warburg, 1949
Letters to Felice (ed. E. Heller & J. Born; tr. J. Stern and E. Duckworth), Secker & Warburg, 1974; Schocken, 1973
The Trial (tr. W. and E. Muir), Secker & Warburg, 1956; Knopf, 1937
KOESTLER, Arthur *Darkness at Noon*, Jonathan Cape, 1940; Bantam, 1970
LAING, R. D. *The Divided Self*, Penguin Books, 1965; Pantheon, 1969
Reason and Violence, Tavistock Publications, 1964
Self and Others, Penguin Books, 1971; Pantheon, 1970
LAWRENCE, D. H. *Aaron's Rod*, William Heinemann, 1954; Viking
The Collected Letters of D. H. Lawrence (ed. Harry T. Moore), William Heinemann, 1962; Viking, 1962
Fantasia of the Unconscious and Psychoanalysis and the Unconscious, Penguin Books, 1971; Viking 1960 (Original edition, Heinemann, 1923)
Kangaroo, William Heinemann, 1955; Viking, 1960
Lady Chatterley's Lover, William Heinemann, 1960; NAL, 1972
The Letters of D. H. Lawrence (ed. Aldous Huxley), William Heinemann, 1932
The Lost Girl, William Heinemann, 1955; Viking, 1968
The Plumed Serpent, William Heinemann, 1955; Knopf, 1951
The Rainbow, William Heinemann, 1954; Viking, 1951
Selected Essays, Penguin Books, 1950
Selected Literary Criticism (ed. Anthony Beal), William Heinemann, 1955; Viking, 1956
Sons and Lovers, William Heinemann, 1963; Viking, 1958
The White Peacock, William Heinemann, 1955; Southern Illinois University Press, 1966
Women in Love, William Heinemann, 1954; Viking, 1920
LEAVIS, F. R. *D. H. Lawrence Novelist*, Chatto & Windus, 1955; Simon & Schuster, 1969
LYND, Helen Merrell *On Shame and the Search for Identity*, Harcourt Brace & World, New York, 1958
McCULLERS, Carson *Reflections in a Golden Eye*, Barrie & Jenkins, 1958; Houghton Mifflin
MacMURRAY, John *The Self as Agent*, Faber & Faber, 1957; Humanities Press, 1969

MAILER, Norman *An American Dream*, André Deutsch, 1965; Dell, 1970
Armies of the Night, Penguin, 1970; NAL, 1971
A Fire on the Moon, Weidenfeld & Nicolson, 1970; NAL, 1971
Marilyn, Coronet Books, 1974; Grosset & Dunlap, 1973
Miami and the Siege of Chicago, Weidenfeld & Nicolson, 1968; NAL, 1971
The Naked and the Dead, André Deutsch, 1960; Holt Rinehart, 1968
Why Are We in Vietnam? Weidenfeld & Nicolson, 1969; Putnam, 1967
MANCHESTER, William *Death of a President*, Michael Joseph, 1967; Harper & Row, 1967
MANN, Thomas *Buddenbrooks*, Secker & Warburg, 1930; Knopf, 1964
Death in Venice, Penguin, 1971; Knopf, 1965
Doctor Faustus, Penguin, 1971; Knopf, 1948
The Magic Mountain (tr. H. T. Lowe-Porter), The English Edition, 1928; Knopf, 1956
Mario and the Magician, Secker & Warburg, 1970
Past Masters and Other Papers (tr. H. T. Lowe-Porter), Martin Secker, 1933; Books for Libraries, 1933
Three Essays (tr. H. T. Lowe-Porter), New York, 1929
Tonio Kröger, Blackwell, 1944; Prentice-Hall, 1961
MASLOW, Abraham H. *Motivation and Personality*, Harper & Row, New York, 1954
MAY, Rollo (ed.) *Existence*, Basic Books, New York, 1958
MÜLLER-VOLLMER, Kurt *Towards a Phenomenological Theory of Literature*, Mouton & Co., The Hague, 1963
MURDOCH, Iris 'Against Dryness', *Encounter*, January 1961
Sartre, Fontana, 1967
NABOKOV, Vladimir *Pale Fire*, Weidenfeld & Nicolson, 1962
ORWELL, George *Nineteen Eighty-Four*, Secker & Warburg, 1949; NAL, 1971
PASSMORE, John *A Hundred Years of Philosophy*, Penguin Books, 1968
POE, Edgar Allan *Tales of Mystery and Imagination*, Pan Books, 1968; Dutton
PROUST, Marcel *Remembrance of Things Past* (tr. C. K. Scott Moncrieff) Chatto & Windus, Uniform Edition, 1941; Random House, 1934
RIVIERE, Joan (ed.) *Developments in Psycho-Analysis*, The Hogarth Press, 1952
ROUSSEAU, Jean-Jacques *Émile*, J. M. Dent, 1974; Dutton, 1974
RUSSELL, Bertrand *History of Western Philosophy*, Allen & Unwin, 1946; Simon & Schuster, 1945
RYLE, Gilbert *The Concept of Mind*, Hutchinson, 1949; Barnes & Noble, 1969
SALINGER, J. D. *The Catcher in the Rye*, Hamish Hamilton, 1951; Bantam, 1970
Franny and Zooey, William Heinemann, 1962; Bantam, 1969
SARTRE, Jean-Paul *Being and Nothingness* (tr. Hazel E. Barnes), Methuen & Co., 1958; Citadel Press, 1965 (Original edition, Paris, 1943)

Existentialism and Humanism (tr. Philip Mairet), Methuen & Co.;
Citadel Press, 1971 (Original edition, Paris, 1946)
Road to Freedom, Hamish Hamilton
Sketch for a Theory of the Emotions (tr. Philip Mairet), Methuen & Co.,
1962 (Original edition, Paris, 1939)
Words, Penguin Books, 1967; Fawcett, 1972 (Original edition, Paris,
1964)
SHATTUCK, Roger *Proust*, Fontana, 1974; Viking, 1974
SMITH, Cecil Woodham *The Great Hunger*, Hamish Hamilton, 1962
The Reason Why, William Heinemann, 1971
STYRON, William *Lie Down in Darkness*, Jonathan Cape, 1970;
Viking, 1957
SULLIVAN, Harry Stack *Conceptions of Modern Psychiatry*, Tavistock
Publications, 1955; Norton, 1953 (Original edition, New York, 1940)
TILLICH, Paul *The Courage to Be*, William Collins, 1962; Yale
University Press, 1952
TOLKIEN, J. R. R. *The Lord of the Rings*, Allen & Unwin, 1969;
Ballantine, 1974
TRILLING, Lionel *The Liberal Imagination*, Secker & Warburg, 1964;
Peter Smith
Sincerity and Authenticity, Oxford University Press, 1972; Harvard
University Press, 1972
UPDIKE, John *Rabbit, Run*, André Deutsch, 1972; Knopf, 1960
WOOLF, Virginia *Jacob's Room*, Hogarth Press, 1945; Harcourt
Brace, 1960
Collected Essays, Vol. 1, Hogarth Press, 1966; Harcourt Brace, 1967
Mrs Dalloway, Hogarth Press, 1950; Harcourt Brace, 1949
Night and Day, Hogarth Press, 1971; Harcourt Brace, 1973
Orlando, Hogarth Press, 1964; Harcourt Brace, 1973
To the Lighthouse, Hogarth Press, 1960; Harcourt Brace, 1949
The Voyage Out, Hogarth Press, 1915; Harcourt Brace, 1960
The Waves, Hogarth Press, 1953
A Writer's Diary, Hogarth Press, 1953; Harcourt Brace, 1973
ZOLA, Emile 'The Naturalist Novel', 1893, *The Nineteenth Century
Novel* (ed. A. Kettle), William Heinemann, 1972

Index

133

134